D1564592

Max Beloff

Gladstone Professor of Government and Public
Administration in the University of Oxford
and Fellow of All Souls College

The Future of British Foreign Policy

Foreword by
Vera Micheles Dean

TAPLINGER PUBLISHING COMPANY
NEW YORK

First published in the United States in 1969 by
Taplinger Publishing Co., Inc.
29 East Tenth Street
New York, New York 10003

Copyright © 1969 by Max Beloff

SBN 8008-3120-9

Library of Congress Catalog Card Number 73–86970

"... I have thought it proper to
represent things as they are in
real truth, rather than as they
are imagined ..."
Niccolò Machiavelli
(*The Prince*, XV).

Printed in Great Britain

Contents

Foreword

THE BRITISH writer and lecturer, Max Beloff, well-known for his many lucid and forthright books on problems of foreign policy, with particular emphasis on Britain, the United States and Europe, undertakes in this volume to assess the future role of Britain, which no longer "rules the waves," and, bereft after World War II of its imperial possessions in Asia, Africa and the Middle East, now ponders the role it could or should play in world affairs.

As Mr Beloff points out, "it has taken a long time for the full impact of the change in Britain's status to make itself felt." And even now that the British, except for some scattered fragments of their former worldwide domain, are restricted territorially to their original island kingdom, they appear uncertain about their current—and future—role in world affairs.

Should Britain, it is variously asked, seek to forge an Anglo-American partnership which might restore at least a semblance of its erstwhile influence? Or should it devise a more versatile—although admittedly precarious—role by combining cooperation in the New World with closer ties to Western Europe, notably, at one and the same time, with West Germany and France, in a political union it had sedulously avoided in past centuries of imperial glory? Or, as a more drastic alternative, should the British, turning their backs on worldwide ties, shift to what Mr Beloff describes as "isolationist little-Englandism with unhealthy overtones of xenophobia and even racialism accompanying it"—as many Britishers appear to be doing in their dismay about non-British citizens of the Commonwealth—notably Indians, who had been brought to East Africa by the

British to build railways and perform other menial tasks—only to be rejected by the newly independent African nations, notably Kenya, and then found, to their distress, that their Commonwealth citizenship did not make them welcome in England where many had sought to start a new life.

Today the British, having discovered with dismay that, contrary to past assumptions, the sun has irrevocably set on the British Empire, face the painful reality that Britain is no longer the center of an imperial Commonwealth. The thorny difficulties of creating a new role for Britain, as Mr Beloff points out, "reflects a party system which no longer corresponds to real divisions in the country and which consequently fails to present the country with the choices that it has to make." Not only is Britain no longer ruler of the seas—it is not even ruler of its own island destiny. Given this situation, the most urgent task, according to Mr Beloff, is to reach an understanding with France "of as complete a kind as possible." Britain should also develop a close association with the Common Market (a task which will require the greatest effort by British industrialists and traders), and assume a position of leadership on the continent by advocating a European federal system.

The theme of this undaunted author can be summed up in the phrase: "There'll always be an England"— even though it is not yet clear just what form the England of tomorrow will take in world affairs.

VERA MICHELES DEAN

Preface

I AM indebted to Mr Brian Crozier the editor of this
series for allowing me to give my book this rather
controversial title and treatment. In what is necessarily a topical study influenced by the outlook of
the moment, it would be pedantic to offer the ap-
paratus of scholarship. Much that I have here set
down in brief I have argued at greater length in
books and articles over the past twenty years: notably in my books: *Foreign Policy and the Democratic
Process* (1955); *Europe and the Europeans* (1957);
The Great Powers (1959); *New Dimensions in Foreign
Policy* (1961); *The United States and the Unity of
Europe* (1963) and *The Great Powers* (1968). But the
main documentation of much of the argument must
await the publication of my large-scale study of the
evolution of Britain's world position in the present
century of which the general title will be *Imperial
Sunset*.

I am most grateful to M. Jacques Freymond, director
of the Graduate Institute of International Studies,
Geneva, for the opportunity of trying out some of
these ideas before an international audience.

I must acknowledge the invaluable help given me
in the research for this book by Miss J. F. Maitland-
Jones who is also working with me on the larger
project. I am much indebted to Mrs Margaret Croft
for the index.

MAX BELOFF

All Souls College, Oxford.
September 1968

1

The Retreat from Empire

THE SENSE of frustration that has increasingly marked the British political scene for the past few years is only indirectly connected with failure or doubts in the sphere of foreign policy. For most people today, as in the past, it is what government does at home—and notably about the economy—that determines their attitude towards it and their electoral behaviour. Nevertheless there is a fairly widespread awareness that there is a connection between the country's economic performance and its management of its relations with other communities. It is also felt, more obscurely but perhaps even more widely, that Britain no longer stands in the world where she did and that this general decline in status is something that affects her citizens as individuals. To talk about the future of foreign policy is to talk about something that goes to the very root of Britain's problems. To get that foreign policy right is the first task of British statesmanship, and it is a necessary precondition of every other measure directed at Britain's recovery.

It is of course equally true that foreign policy, if it is to be successful, must rest on healthy economic and political foundations. Circumscribed though it must be by considerations of power, foreign policy is also dependent upon psychological factors. A country that is a prey to self-doubt and defeatism is unlikely to have a government that will make the right decisions or to give it proper support when it does so. The more democratic its institutions, the more a country will depend on its citizens' understanding of the issues at stake.

Whatever may be thought of specific decisions made by British governments since the end of the

Second World War, the main charge against them is their responsibility for helping to conceal the true nature of the events themselves. To say that Britain's world status has diminished and that this is an inevitable consequence of developments outside her control is to repeat the most familiar of platitudes; although one is well aware that there are quarters in which this would be denied, and in which it is thought that by some exertion of will-power alone, the tables could be turned and Britain's Great Power status be miraculously restored. But what is worth saying as a prelude to an inquiry about what the future may have in store, is that it has taken a long time for the full impact of the change in Britain's status to make itself felt.

Indeed, very recently it was possible to take the view that Britain was going to prove an exception to the general rule that the loss of Empire and of the world position that it brings has an immediate, far-reaching and often disruptive effect upon the nation concerned. It has normally had a direct impact upon social attitudes and political institutions alike. If Britain had provided such an exception, it would have been paradoxical in the extreme; for of all modern imperial powers, it has been Britain for whom the imperial element has been the most important. It has been indeed an essential constituent of Britain's image of itself. For Belgium, for Holland—despite the size and wealth of her East Indian possessions—even for France, overseas Empire was a useful appendage and not much more; the core of their being lay elsewhere. And this was even truer of Italy and Germany. One has to go back to Spain of the sixteenth to the eighteenth centuries to find a truer parallel to the British case; and some would say that Spain has not even now fully recovered from the trauma of her imperial catastrophe.

But Britain has not in fact provided an exception to the rule. The shock is there all right; but it has been a delayed shock, and the delay has been a harmful one, because it has prevented the emergence of a full understanding of what has happened, and of what in the new conditions Britain's role might usefully be. We often hear it claimed as a virtue that Britain, unlike some of Europe's other ex-imperial powers, is at least outward-looking and has not turned its back upon the rest of the world out of pique that it can no longer hope to control its destinies. And there is, no doubt, some truth in this, as whatever may be the case elsewhere there are very real reasons why Britain's fortunes should be regarded as interdependent with those of much of the rest of the world. But there are dangers in the outward look as well. A great deal of thought has been given to the impact of the winding-up of the Empire upon the ex-imperial and colonial territories; there has been much interest in academic as well as political quarters in the fortunes of the "New States". But there has been much less interest in the fact that the change has been of equal magnitude where Britain itself has been concerned, and much less inventiveness in respect of institutional alterations that this change might render necessary. As a result, we now face the opposite danger, the danger of a sudden and total revulsion against anything that reminds us of past advantages and past glories, a sudden shift into an isolationist little-Englandism with unhealthy overtones of xenophobia and even racialism accompanying it.

The dangers inherent in the sudden realization of what the situation is should not, however, provide an excuse for refusing to face the facts. Anyhow, that option is no longer open, and one reason is that it is not only the politicians—with some assistance from publicists of various kinds—who have been responsible for prolonging our illusions. Other countries have contributed also; for there have been good arguments in their view in favour of cushioning Britain against the full impact of reality. This has been true above all of the United States, the natural and inevitable successor to Britain in many of Britain's former roles —however unwilling the United States may have been to play that particular part. It has suited the United States—at least until very recently—to encourage the view that Britain could still play a Great Power role in the old sense. In part this has been due to the clear American dislike of being left with no proper interlocutor on her own side of the great ideological divide; in part it has been due to a hope that Britain could still sustain some of the burden of common defence, and thus take some of the load off American shoulders. But there has also been the perfectly simple and straightforward reason that over most of the issues arising in world politics since the war, the British and Americans have in fact been closer in their assessment and reactions than have the Americans and the western Europeans. It has not simply been a matter of the United States encouraging Britain to trust in the validity of the "special relationship" by engaging in consultations with her upon a more or less equal footing; there has also been positive assistance from the Americans in the field of nuclear armaments, and in sustaining the position of sterling. Nor in the latter aspect of the job have the Americans been alone. Sterling's world role may be irksome to Britain's industrial competitors, but so long as it exists there is a powerful incentive for other countries to make it easier for Britain to maintain it. But here again, the extent to which Britain has profited by the enlightened self-interest of others is very rarely cited by politicians who claim all the credit for the country's successes, and blame external forces for all its failures.

The spell has now been broken. Too much has happened for there to be any illusions about the world being an easy place for Britain to earn a living in; and the period of cushioning may have come to an end as well. Gratitude in politics is short-lived at the best of times. The credit Britain earned by standing alone against the Nazi monster was largely dissipated by her rejection of European leadership in the immediately post-war years. And now there is a generation growing up in Europe—as in Britain—for whom the whole Hitlerite episode is only a bit of past history. Just as "Suez" destroyed the British belief that in the last resort the Americans could always be with us, so Viet Nam has shown the Americans that there are aspects of their world-task as they see it where Britain cannot be counted on for assistance, or indeed for full sympathy or understanding. Both Europeans and Americans will henceforth treat Britain in the light of what she is, not of what she has been, even though the newer Commonwealth countries seem more prone to judge Britain in the light of her "imperialist" past than as a country with something still to offer to them in their new status.

It would be interesting to speculate on what events have most contributed to the sudden tearing down of the veils between Britain's true position and the way in which her people have perceived it. Different people would make up different lists and give different relative weights to their components. But all the lists would probably include the following; the double rejection of Britain's attempt to enter the European Economic Community (which was a reminder that she was no longer so much wanted in Europe as to be able to impose her own terms); the realization that although British ministers might still scurry off to Washington whenever a decent excuse presented itself, they were no longer getting the red-carpet treatment from President Johnson that had been theirs in the days of his four immediate predecessors; the interruption in Rhodesia of the smooth discarding of imperial responsibilities and the acceptance of United Nations, that is of foreign opinion, as a decisive factor in the handling of a British overseas community; the sad need to make a breach with the previous policy of the open door for Commonwealth citizens in this country, and the inability to find a criterion for restriction that was neither overtly racialist nor yet a violation of the instinctive and understandable expectations of Australians, New Zealanders and Canadians; the discovery that the United Nations itself, in the creation of whose institutions Britain had played a major part, was now a forum in which Britain could hardly ever hope for an impartial let alone a friendly hearing. Suddenly the British have come to feel that they are being kicked around; it is not a feeling to which their history has accustomed them and that they resent it is inevitable. But policy cannot be built upon resentments, only upon facts. What are the facts?

The question is not a simple one, for the facts in the case are of different kinds. The most obvious are those concerning Britain's contemporary situation in relation to other powers and groups of powers, and these can to some extent be treated objectively on the basis of statistical and other material. But there is also the question of which desires of the community can be regarded as touching external policy, and the degree of effort and sacrifice the community will be willing to make in order to achieve them. One has, as a corollary of this question, to ask what institutions exist to make it possible for such objectives to be defined and put into execution. Finally, we have to arrive at an even more speculative assessment of the objectives of other communities and of the extent to which British policy can be reconciled with them, or can only achieve its aims by thwarting them.

To put the questions in this way is to make certain assumptions that not everyone would accept, and it is therefore necessary to begin by spelling them out. The first assumption is that the United Kingdom is a political unit whose motive force is provided by the collective desires of its citizens and that the business of its government is to pursue these as far as lies within its power. It could be argued—and it is power-fully argued in some quarters—that this should be regarded as a transient state of affairs and that the principal objective of British policy should be to merge the United Kingdom into some larger political unit; at which point, of course, British foreign policy would cease to be a meaningful concept, just as one cannot talk of Texan foreign policy. But for the moment this objective has not been attained, nor is there at present any wider unit to which British interests are or should be subordinate.

It is necessary to say this because there has been a good deal of discussion based on the contrary assumption. There have been those who believe that British policy could somehow be based upon the United Nations, just as their predecessors argued that it could be based upon the League of Nations. It has not been made clear that the United Nations is itself one of the instrumentalities through which one can try to make policy effective, and no more than that. A preference for the use of the United Nations machinery over other alternative possibilities is perfectly respectable, but it does not obviate the need for deciding what the policy should be that is thus pursued, nor indeed would there be a wholehearted acquiescence in the idea that the solution of problems with which Britain is directly concerned should be left to be decided by majorities in the General Assembly or even the Security Council.

More important has been the view that the United Kingdom is not itself to be thought of as having a policy of its own but only as the exponent of the policy of a wider system, the Commonwealth. British governments in making policy have been expected to take into account not only the benefits to be derived from such policy by the inhabitants of the British

Isles, but also the consequences for inhabitants of other countries in the Commonwealth, and of course for the remaining British dependencies. It was held, indeed, that the substance of policy was less important than whether or not it conduced to the health and perpetuation of the Commonwealth system. This point of view also still subsists in some quarters.

Between these two ways of questioning the right and capacity of Britain to follow an independent policy based upon enlightened self-interest, there is of course a major difference. The point of view that stresses the United Nations is based upon expectations about the future; the priority given to the Commonwealth rests upon an interpretation of the past, and of its consequences for the present. As an interpretation of the past the view has much to commend it. It is undeniable that for a long period of time it was the foreign policy of an Empire that British statesmen rightly saw themselves as conducting. There might be arguments as to how far Britain should let itself get embroiled abroad through the pursuit of imperial aims, or as to how far parts of the Empire aspiring to self-government should share the burdens of the common defence, but apart from a minority of Little Englanders most people in public life saw the system as a single whole and accepted the view that Britain's interests were first and foremost in its maintenance.

The acquisition by the old "Dominions" of autonomy in foreign as well as domestic matters which marked the transformation of Empire into Commonwealth did not at once put an end to this fundamental attitude of mind. It meant that the "Dominions" had if they wished to use it a more considerable say in what Britain's foreign policy should be, and their tendency was to try to make it as negative and cautious as possible except where their territorial or other interests were directly involved.

In the period between the two world wars, which was the period in which the Commonwealth ideology was most effective, the main concern of Commonwealth statesmen such as Mackenzie King and General Smuts was to prevent Britain from undertaking responsibilities in Europe, either through the League of Nations or directly, which might drag them into war. But when the war came, the Commonwealth still fought it as a system, even though there were frictions (notably between the United Kingdom and Australia) as to the priorities to be allotted to the different fronts. From the United Kingdom point of view, Burma and Malaya, Ethiopia and the Western desert figured as prominently in the war news as Europe itself. The vision of an embattled island may have been the principal source of the inspiration upon which Winston Churchill relied to see that the British people came through the dark days of 1940–1; but the island was not alone. The Russians and the Americans might wait too for external attack to force them into war, but the Dominions by their own volition, India and the colonial territories through a final exertion of the British fiat, were in the war from the start.

It is therefore understandable that the immediately post-war generation of British statesmen, all of whom had served with Churchill, should carry over into the new era the feeling that Britain was not simply a European power of the middle rank hopelessly overshadowed by the United States and the Soviet Union, but the centre of an Empire-Commonwealth, entitled to speak to the giants on equal terms and to regard her continental neighbours, ravaged by war and demoralized by defeat and internal strife, as something less than equal.

Nevertheless they were wrong. In their very different ways the United States and the Soviet Union were Great Powers just because they were ruled by governments which could (despite the real degree of federalism in the United States and the nominal element of federalism in the Soviet Union) muster for national purposes all the resources within their borders. The British government was rapidly to lose its power to make use at will of any resources outside those of the home islands, and there could be no substitute in mere arrangements for consultation for the absence of any institutional framework for the system as a whole.

The early defeats at the hands of the Japanese in 1941–2 and the narrowness of the margin by which the Middle East was held had made it clear that the defence of the system single-handed was beyond Britain's powers; and the recovery of what had been lost was clearly due to the adding of the Soviet Union and the United States to the list of Germany's and Japan's enemies. The Soviet Union was inevitably and by definition opposed to the continued existence of the British Empire, and the United States (through the mouth of President Roosevelt) had made it clear, even before the war ended, that although the independence of Britain (as of the remainder of western Europe) was an American interest, the defence of the British Empire, and the maintenance of the Commonwealth system, were not.

Any attempt to restrain the progress of ideas of autonomy or independence within the Empire would thus have to be pursued in a hostile environment, as the French and the Dutch were also to find, and there would be no support from outside for any methods that might be tried to strengthen the system through economic or other means. Indeed the hostility of the United States to preferential economic arrangements within the Commonwealth went back as far as the Ottawa agreements of 1932 (and even beyond them) and had never been abandoned.

Much was made of the fact that the concessions to the local nationalist movements were made with good grace and without the rearguard actions that marked the dissolution of the French and Dutch Empires. Much too was made of the fact that most of the former imperial territories and colonies chose to remain in the Commonwealth, and even if republican in constitution to accept the British sovereign as head of the Commonwealth.

What was less appreciated was that the new and enlarged Commonwealth, though inheriting the mechanisms of consultation of its predecessor (the Commonwealth of the Balfour formula and the Statute of Westminster), would not use them in the same way or with the same results, because the governing assumption of an ultimate identity of interests and of the desirability of retaining the Commonwealth tie for its own sake was now lacking. The first main political problem for Britain in the post-war period was the forging of instruments of resistance to the expansion of Soviet communism; by and large the newer members of the Commonwealth challenged the need for such action and refused to implicate themselves in it. The second main problem was the re-shaping of British policy in relation to the apparently growing consolidation of Western Europe; the prospect of such reshaping left the countries of the Commonwealth (including its older members) either indifferent or hostile.

For their part the newer Commonwealth countries were primarily concerned to accelerate the process of decolonization and to secure the maximum of aid from Britain to help them in their pursuit of economic growth and modernization. From this angle the Commonwealth was merely a means through which pressure could be exerted on Britain to use her own strength in pursuit of their aims even past the point at which Britain thought them feasible. And such pressures themselves were perhaps thought of as less important than what could be done through the United Nations.

So far therefore from the Commonwealth, as now consituted, being a net asset to Britain in the sense of adding to her available resources, it had become (apart from certain bilateral economic arrangements) a net liability both in respect of the material claims made upon her and in respect of the limitations imposed upon her freedom of action. Some sympathizers with the new Commonwealth countries and their claims have defended this situation on the ground that Britain (like other imperial countries) owes reparation to her ex-possessions for economic gains allegedly made at their expense during the colonial period.

On the British side the most obvious legacy of the

earlier Empire-Commonwealth has been in the field of domestic rather than of foreign policy, though it is a subject which has obvious overtones in international relations as well. Because of the assumptions made about the unity of the Commonwealth and the status of citizens of Commonwealth countries, Britain although a country which has imposed controls over immigration for many decades has not until recently extended them to the countries of the Commonwealth. With the opportunities for employment created by post-war economic policies this open door policy produced a large-scale immigration into Britain from the West Indies, India, Pakistan and parts of Africa.

The social difficulties resulting from the pace at which immigration was taking place, and the vision of the almost limitless pool of possible immigrants particularly from the Indian sub-continent, created a demand for limitation which it proved impossible to resist. Nevertheless, before this could become national policy there was much heart-searching on the part of people who would not have thought of calling into question the limitations long imposed on would-be migrants from Europe. It is true that it is difficult to distinguish concern for the Commonwealth from the sensitivity to accusations of race-prejudice that is characteristic today of much of the opinion-forming class in Britain. Indeed in order to avoid accusations of racial prejudice it was necessary to make the controls equally applicable to the citizens of the old "White Dominions" from which no mass-immigration was to be expected and from whose citizens, when they did come in search of employment, no problems were to be expected. The indignation that such controls inspired, particularly in Australia, and Britain's imperviousness to it indicate how important the "new" Commonwealth has been in shaping Britain's international attitudes.

It is typical of the illusory aspect of the Commonwealth idea that other members of the Commonwealth have not thought that they should give preferential treatment to citizens of Commonwealth countries as such, and that they have always regarded full control over immigration as an essential element in their autonomy or sovereignty. The case of the Kenya Asians is highly revealing. In order to make Kenyan independence and African rule palatable to the Asian minority, Britain undertook to give British passports to those who chose to exercise this option. When affected by the pressure for the Africanization of the Kenyan economy, they began to seek to put their status to use by migrating to Britain, it was found necessary to limit their access; and it was then made plain that India, their country of ultimate origin, in no way felt itself bound to offer them an alternative refuge.

A further legacy of the Commonwealth, and one more directly in the external field, has been the development of British policy towards South Africa and Rhodesia. It is assumed by most members of the Commonwealth that Britain has a particular responsibility for bringing about the downfall of regimes based upon white ascendancy, whether inside or outside the Commonwealth. And to a large extent this argument is accepted, as shown in relation both to sanctions against Rhodesia and to the sale of arms to

South Africa. It is clear that other countries which may have no more affection than the British have for the principles or practices of the South African and Rhodesian regimes see no reason why they should inflict economic losses upon their own people to help displace them, nor is much pressure exerted upon them to do so. And even where colour is not involved, as in the Nigerian civil war, it is obvious that both sides expected a positive attitude by Britain that was not demanded of other powers.

It would therefore seem that, given the kind of issues with which Britain has in fact been confronted and given the existence of the forum for pressure upon her provided by the United Nations, there has in fact been no perceptible difference in relations between Britain and those countries which, like India and Kenya, chose to remain in the Commonwealth, as compared with those which like Burma and the Sudan chose self-exclusion. The amalgamation of the foreign and commonwealth services into a single diplomatic service and the merging of the Foreign Office and the Commonwealth Relations Office into a single department may be looked at as marking an implicit assent by the British government to the force of this argument.

If the first assumption is that Britain itself and not the Commonwealth is the focus of such a study as this, the second is that Britain today is not and cannot be a Great Power in the traditional sense. It is again important to state this assumption both because it is sometimes disputed—as General de Gaulle has disputed it in the analogous case of France—and because important consequences flow from it.

Even if nuclear weapons had not been invented it is doubtful whether the late nineteenth and early twentieth-century pattern of quite a number of Great Powers could have continued into the present period. If the creation and maintenance of multi-national Empires (except in the case of Russia) was no longer possible, the development of industrial societies of the modern kind was bound to put a premium on nations of continental size; size of population and variety of resources combined with centralized direction would settle where power lay. The rise of the United States and Russia to world dominance had long been foreseen. But with the advent of nuclear weapons the gap between the Great and the Medium Powers was rendered unbridgeable.

It was not originally clear that this would be the case. And there have indeed been arguments to the contrary; it has been held—and the French still hold —that nuclear weapons are equalizing in their effect, in that, once possessed of them, a State has it in its power to threaten unacceptable damage even to the mightiest enemy. But though this may have been true at one stage in the development of nuclear weapons, it is certainly not true now. The increased sophistication of missile-systems both for offence and defence—and their increased cost—has ruled out the possibility of medium size powers remaining in the nuclear race to any effect where the Great Powers are concerned. The only possible use to the lesser powers of nuclear weapons is in respect of their relations with each other, and then only in the unlikely event of the Great Powers disinteresting themselves from a particular regional conflict. It is sometimes said that the lesser powers have the additional possibility within alliances of forcing their major allies into a nuclear war by themselves escalating a conflict. But this is only another way of saying that they can commit national suicide if they wish, since it is hard to see how they could hope to escape total retribution whatever the fate of their Great Power ally.

Whether some technical revolution as awe-inspiring as the nuclear revolution itself could redress the balance is something upon which we do not need to speculate. All that one can say is that Britain, despite its possession of a nuclear weapon system, is not in a position to play a Great Power role and that this is or should have been obvious at least since the Suez affair of 1956.

From this assumption three possible consequences could be drawn. Britain could decide that in such circumstances the interests of the British people would best be satisfied by becoming part of some Great Power parting with sovereignty for good for the sake of a voice in the disposition and utilization of its nuclear weapons; what this would mean in practice is joining a European political community which would itself be equipped to act as a Great Power in the Russian or American sense. In fact, even if such were a desirable aim, the possibility of achieving it in the present temper of Western Europe seems so remote that it hardly needs be raised in order to be dismissed. For such a community would require not only resources on the Russian and American scale—these except in terms of space are perhaps present—but also a willingness to use them in the same way, and of this there is no evidence at all, as a glance at the element of defence expenditure in the budgets of the countries concerned immediately makes clear.

A second possible consequence would be to continue even more determinedly on the line that Britain has pursued ever since the war, that of relying on a quasi-permanent alliance system. It could be argued that just as isolation, and acting as a balancing factor between rival groupings, was a plausible and for some time a profitable policy for Britain in its period as a Great Power, a policy of total commitment to one side in a bi-polar world is the correct response to the new situation.

The third consequence is a variant of the second. It can be argued that if the security of a medium-power is of direct concern to a Great Power no alliance is needed by the former, that a neutral State can equally well profit by the determination of the two rival Great Powers not to let the other gain a decisive advantage. It could even be argued that this would be the cheapest course of action, although Swedish experience would not bear this out.

The difficulty with this approach is that the successful examples of it that can be quoted relate to countries (like Sweden) whose interests are geographically confined and relatively easy to specify. What is characteristic of Britain in the post-imperial age is that although her resources are those of a medium power only, her interests remain world-wide, to some extent more so than in the case of the two super-Powers themselves. And one assumption of this study is that these interests are not adventitious or easily discarded, but on the contrary essential elements in Britain's health, both material and psychological.

The final assumption is implicit in what has already been said. It is that power and influence are inextricably intertwined and that in the last resort the international community like the domestic community depends on the ability to use force. In domestic affairs force is normally monopolized by the State, and if matters are properly managed it should never need to appear in the foreground; most of the community's functioning depends upon consent. In international affairs, force is distributed, if unequally, among formally independent but normally interdependent sovereign units, having with each other relations that partake at once of competition and collaboration. The effort to keep force in the background depends upon the exercise of self-restraint—a self-restraint which needs to be bolstered by fear and other aspects of self-interest.

Britain is not exempt in any way from these rules. As a unit in the international system, she is bound by its rules and subject to its servitudes. It is no good saying that having shed Great Power status, she has no further need to be able to assert her will, or that the absence of any motives for aggression on her part allows her to neglect precautions against the aggressive or acquisitive impulses of others. Even those whose only aim in life is to cultivate their garden need to attend to the fences.

And although the reputation of a country upon which its influence depends does not wholly derive from its material strength, it can never be unrelated to it. To say that Britain should achieve some objective—in the field of disarmament for instance—by "setting an example" shows an unfamiliarity with the

working of a state-system. A lead will be followed
only when other countries feel that it is in their interests to do so.

   If this view is contested in Britain today—especially
though not exclusively by the young—the reason is
once again to be found largely in the time-lag between
the alteration in Britain's world position and the
general appreciation of it. Attitudes proper to the citizens of a world power are carried over into the new
situation. The left-wing intellectuals who talk of
Britain's duty to set an example to the world are just
as much the heirs of empire as the most belligerent
protagonist of national interest on the extreme Right.
And it would perhaps be surprising if this were not
the case.

   When Britain decided that civilization could not
tolerate the slave-trade, she was largely successful in
extirpating it because she was the great naval power
of the time and could make it her business to enforce
the international consensus on the matter by action
against any recalcitrant. She cannot today enforce the
ending of slavery itself or of the smuggling of slaves
where this still goes on; still less can she make herself
responsible for enforcing other general principles such
as those of racial equality where these are defied. Similarly, at the time of the Don Pacifico debate Palmerston could assert the principle of *civis romanus sum*
because it was indeed the case that over much of the
world Britain had the capacity to assert the rights of
her individual citizens where these appeared to have
been violated. Today she is compelled to pocket her
pride and to compensate them (if they are compensated at all) out of the pockets of her own taxpayers,

rather than out of the resources of the wrong-doers.

Indeed one could say that it is sometimes the vain pursuit of the wider goals that hampers the attainment of the more modest ones. For the greatest danger from the survival of imperial attitudes is that words will now be used not as indications of action but as a substitute for it. Instead of "speak softly but carry a big stick"—which is the counsel of prudence—the exhortation we get is "throw the stick away and shout as loudly as possible." And that is a doctrine as dangerous as it is undignified.

All this is not to say that we can return into some cynical version of *Realpolitik* whereby foreign policy can be carried out irrespective of the country's nobler ideals and aspirations, or that the failure of the international community to develop higher moral standards should actually be applauded. The demand for civilizing international society, for having more and more of its activities subjected to an agreed code of law and acceptable peaceful procedures—these are demands which are heard in many different forms from many different quarters of the globe. A government that wholly ignored their force would be in danger of cutting itself off from the sympathies of an important and growing section of the human race, and these demands are powerfully reinforced by the new deadliness that our scientists have added to the age-old horrors of war.

Where British power or influence can be made to function in favour of such progress towards a more peaceful international society it is incumbent upon a British government to act in this sense. But not every appeal made to it in the name of peaceful progress is genuine; sometimes such an appeal may be a simple disguise for sheer acquisitiveness. Each such appeal must be judged on its merits.

In judging particular proposals in the field of external policy we have then not one but two criteria. In the first place, we must ask whether the proposal conduces to a measurable benefit to the inhabitants of the British isles. In the second place, we must ask whether the methods we employ to resolve whatever the issue may be help to promote the kind of international society in which we would feel safer and happier, or the reverse. We must not be too certain that these criteria will never conflict, nor that we can always be sure as to which deserves priority. Much of the sequel will help to illustrate this standing and inevitable predicament. Neither the making of foreign policy nor the passing of judgement upon it is as easy as some would have us believe.

2

Defining the National Interest

THE APPROACH that we have outlined must depend
for its validity on the belief that the national interest
can be ascertained, and that the first task of the policy-
maker or policy-critic is to define it. It can only be
defined in relation to a particular State, because, although there may be objectives that many or even all
States share, these will normally be of a degree of
generality that give no guidance to the actual makers
of foreign policy. Furthermore, in so far as their
achievement depends upon the actions of many States,
the actions of the State with which one is concerned
may be marginal in respect of success or failure; and
failure may produce disillusion and uncertainty.

When in the inter-war period it was commonly
stated that the policy of Britain was one of "peace",
this was an example of precisely this kind. For, as
events were to show, the choice between peace and
war was not something in Britain's hands alone, and
the degree of preference for peace over war was strictly
relative to the issues involved. A similar ambiguity
affects declarations to the effect that British policy is
a "League of Nations" or "United Nations" policy.

It may be argued that, provided the objective is desirable, the attempt to pursue it is worth making
irrespective of the likelihood of success. But this is not
so. It is of the utmost importance in any State, and
particularly in a democracy, that people should have
confidence in the general direction of affairs and nothing so easily destroys this confidence as the feeling
that the country is pursuing some line of policy whose
fulfilment is principally dependent on the will or even
the whim of others. Even when the issues at stake are
only dimly apprehended and when failure has not the

dire consequences of leading to war, there is some degree of self-identification between the citizen and the State of which he is a member. However desirable British adhesion to the Treaty of Rome may still be thought, it would be unwise of any government to risk a situation in which negotiations could again be brought to an end by the veto of a foreign government, because of the domestic repercussions which such an affront would almost certainly produce.

One could go further and say that in any democracy, indeed in any nation where the power of the State rests on anything but naked force, the principal national interest in foreign policy is the maintenance of national unity in its support. Any policy which deeply divides a nation should if possible be avoided. It may be impossible that agreement should be reached because the subject is one to which honest men can apply criteria that are irreconcilable—particularly if a moral issue enters into it or is believed to do so. But every effort ought to be made to reach agreement and to see whether a greater knowledge of the facts of a situation would not lead to a somewhat greater degree of consensus than at first seemed possible.

The important thing is that policy-makers should take into account the fact that division at home is something itself so damaging that if necessary a high price should be paid to avoid it. Energies that are dissipated in a debate over foreign policy may be needed for more constructive purposes, and important things that are within reach of a country may be left undone because of external preoccupations. How difficult this principle may be to follow in the British case will concern us later, but it should be easier in the future than it was in the past, because the only community whose opinions need to be taken into account is the one at home. There is none of the complication which in the inter-war years was introduced by the need also to take into account the likely movement of opinion in other countries of the Commonwealth.

What may divide a community is not only differences about the external environment, but also the picture which it has of itself. As we have seen, in the British case there is the overlay of a self-portrait done at the height of the imperial era in British history which tends to obscure the humbler lineaments of to-day. A country's opinion of itself may also depend upon the standards of comparison which are in use at any particular time and here fashions change. If we take the United States as a measuring-rod—and in many quarters it is almost a matter of instinct to do so—we may see ourselves as relatively poor, technically backward, managerially incompetent. If we take the vast majority of countries in the world we find ourselves wealthy, efficient, progressive. By some standards we are the victims of an ever-increasing bureaucratic domination with little scope given for individual initiative and little opportunity to call our rulers into account. By comparison with eastern Europe we enjoy an unbelievable degree of personal freedom and much opportunity to criticize and even change our rulers.

But it should be possible to get agreement on certain facts which are essential for an understanding of the needs of our foreign policy. We must begin with the simplest of them, namely, that the British position from the economic point of view is at once unique and precarious. The standard of living which we take for granted, and which most people think should rise at an even greater rate than it has been doing, is the result of a series of historical events which have not been reproduced anywhere else. By reason of Britain's early start with industrialization and the decision to sacrifice other possible sources of strength—a large agricultural population for instance—to the development of industry, its markets, and its financing, we have come in the mid-twentieth century to occupy a position which it is unlikely anyone would have thought of planning.

The population of the British Isles was allowed to grow to a point where it became dependent upon imported foodstuffs, and its industry flourished on imported raw materials. And these have had to be paid for partly by the sales of industrial products abroad and more particularly, since the early industrial lead was lost, by earnings on shipping, insurance, investment and banking operations. It was of the essence of this network of international transactions that it was a world-wide one and not directed towards any particular geographical region.

We do not need to go into the vexed question of the extent to which the Empire itself was the product of the drive to expand and safeguard trading and financial opportunities. All one can say is that the post-imperial era has not so far seen any substantial change in the extent to which the country depends upon them. It does not matter therefore very much to this part of the argument that the specific difficulties in the balance of payments from which Britain has suffered since the war are in part attributable to noncommercial forms of overseas expenditure—defence in particular, or to a legacy of the war itself—the sterling balances. The real thing that matters is the enormously high proportion that foreign trade and investment still plays in the British economy by comparison with other countries. For this involves both direct physical vulnerability (as was shown by Britain's nearness to disaster as a result of the submarine campaigns of the two world wars) and also an indirect and more diffuse vulnerability to any other form of interference with the normal course of international commerce wherever it may occur.

It is because so much of the world's trade is, or has been, British that sterling has been an international trading currency and that London has been an important money-market. And this means a further vulnerability to any upset in world credit arrangements, any rapid movements in the terms of trade, any threat to the viability of other economies, and to economic mismanagement by other major countries.

Vulnerability of this kind implies a high degree of interdependence whose consequences people naturally find irksome. But since this degree of interdependence is inextricably bound up with the foundations of the British economy itself, it is hard to see how it can be altered without a veritable revolution which might leave us worse off than before. We could of course achieve a much higher degree of self-sufficiency if we were willing to pay the price of a lower standard of living; but except in wartime this has not been a proposition that has seriously commended itself to any government or to the electorate.

Some of the implications of this situation are primarily domestic and have only secondary repercussions upon foreign policy. It is obvious, for instance, that an industrial economy so situated needs a high degree of flexibility so as to be able to transfer resources particularly labour to other lines of output as markets for earlier staples disappear. For nearly a century there have been complaints that this process has not been fast enough, that Britain was for instance using political leverage within the Empire to preserve traditional outlets for her goods rather than allowing market forces to dictate the redeployment of her resources.

It is possible of course for such leverage to be exercised in a non-imperial situation—as some of the member countries of the Common Market, notably France, have shown in regard to agricultural policy, for instance. But the degree of leverage that Britain now enjoys is not very high anywhere, and our ability to compete is largely a question of the comparative efficiency of our own industry. Whatever inroads may be made on the competitive principle internally, in international economic relations, the laws of competition still operate, even when state-trading is involved as in our relations with the eastern *bloc*. Price, quality and credit terms decide results; although both customers' habits and marketing techniques have a role to play.

Foreign policy is affected by this situation in a number of ways. In the first place, as has been seen, what matters most to Britain about the international environment is that it should be stable; that the world's sea and air routes and highways should be open, that international contracts should be fulfilled, and methods available for enforcing them, that investments should be made without fear of confiscation, and above all that there should be peace. It is hard to think of any spot on the globe where civil disorder, let alone all-out war, would not be detrimental to some British interest.

The difficulty is not so much that this fact is denied —though there are some people in whose minds it does not figure very prominently—as that while it is true (if to a lesser degree) of the position of many other countries, they may decline to recognize the fact, and either actually help to promote trouble, for their own reasons or at best remain passive, and rely on Britain to make the necessary outlay required to preserve the peace.

While Britain has twice within just over a decade suffered economically from the closure of the Suez canal, the second closure was less important than the first because measures had meanwhile been taken by important countries which made it less significant to them—the building and purchase of larger tankers, for instance. But the Soviet Union and India have been important sufferers on the latter occasion, yet both have been involved in policies likely to promote the tension in the Middle East from which the closure of the canal resulted, the Soviet Union by supplying the means for Egyptian belligerence, India by ministering to Nasser's self-esteem.

Again, no other western European country has shown any disposition to take steps to guarantee the continued output of the oil of the Persian Gulf after the British withdrawal which is all too likely to place it in jeopardy. And in these circumstances it has of course been an open question—now decided in the negative—as to whether Britain should continue to play a policing role which other countries show by their actions they regard as otiose.

Perhaps they are right; but one's feeling is that despite all that has been happening in the "Third World", and even in some of their own cities, the advanced industrial countries (communist as well as capitalist) still under-rate the extent to which modern industrial societies are vulnerable to minority-fomented disorder, to riot, sabotage and guerrilla warfare, and fail to see how ill-equipped they are to respond to it, particularly psychologically.

The second aspect of this situation in which foreign policy is involved is the constant need to diversify as much as possible both our sources of supply and our markets. Interdependence is only a tolerable situation when one is involved with a great many other countries; otherwise one's margin of freedom and susceptibility to blackmail is too high. The problem in Britain's case is complicated by the financial factor. In the case of oil, for instance, there have always been diverse sources to draw from, but some of them involved an outlay in dollars while others did not. And dollars spent on oil were not available for supplies which could only be obtained in hard currency. In respect of markets, the same applies in reverse. There are countries where one can sell but only by accepting a virtual barter arrangement for goods which one might not put high on one's list otherwise, or by extending credit on not very profitable terms.

The search for and exploitation of new business opportunities is principally one for individual business firms. But the government has both negative and positive powers; negative in the sense of being able to prohibit certain dealings because of an over-riding political consideration or to discourage businessmen from going forward with them in the various ways open to it; positive by giving support in the shape of favourable credit or taxation arrangements.

The political aspect has been intermittently a prominent one because of the "cold war". How far in a conflict of this kind is the conception of trading with the enemy applicable? On this subject there have been differences of opinion between Britain and some of her allies, notably the United States. These differences reveal in part a rather different attitude to the "cold war" itself, because the ideological aspects of it have never bulked so large in British as in American opinion. In part, however, they arise from the fact that the United States can more easily afford to sacrifice potential markets for its goods or services, both because of the greater strength of its economy and because of the lesser importance to it of international trade as a whole.

The upshot has been an apparent compromise in which agreements have been reached among the members of the Atlantic Alliance to refrain from selling goods to communist countries of direct importance to their war-making capability. But there can be wide discrepancies as to what goods come under this head, and there have been distinctions between what has been thought permissible in the case of Soviet Russia and eastern Europe and in the case of Cuba which the United States regards and treats as not merely a potential enemy, but an actual one.

Nor are such differences of opinion necessarily confined to the purchase or sale of goods; there is also the question of the extent to which British firms should participate in building up the economic potential of the Soviet bloc itself by entering into agreements for the construction of industrial plant or for technical assistance. Can Britain afford to take a more rigid line than her European competitors? No magic formula exists by which to answer questions of this kind. The need to diversify Britain's economic outlets and to enhance her economic, and hence political, strength may have to be balanced against the damage which particular steps may involve for the fabric of her alliances—unless one is prepared to write the latter off entirely. Business and politics cannot be put into separate compartments however much some businessmen and some politicians would like this to be the case.

Nor is it only in respect of Britain's alliances that there are limitations upon her commercial freedom of action. Opinion at home may be such as to force a government to prevent certain forms of trade with some countries, or all trade with others. British policy towards Rhodesia since UDI would be an example of the latter, and the refusal to sell arms to South Africa of the former. There may be circumstances in which such demands will be resisted, as in the case of the supply of arms to Nigeria during the Nigerian civil war, although it may be argued that here the reasons were political rather than economic. It may be said of course that all these three cases are exceptional, because they are all related to countries that are or have been within the Commonwealth, so that policy towards them is likely to be much more ideological in character and much more controversial than in the case of foreign countries in the full sense. But there is no doubt that British opinion is very ready to manifest hostility to regimes which defy its current standards of acceptability, and that sections of it will always be looking for ways in which economic action can be used to the detriment of such regimes.

It is of course easier to do so when the direct economic interests appear to be those of a small and identifiable group, such as the suppliers of arms, as the loss of a market to a particular industry is only indirectly connected in people's minds with their own economic well-being. It is also true that ideologically-motivated action of this kind tends to be demanded for only a limited period—indignation about the misdeeds of foreigners is difficult to keep up for long at a time.

Relations between Britain and Spain illustrate both these points. During and immediately after the Spanish Civil War and in the early post-war period, it was easy to command support for limiting trade with Spain or taking other hostile measures. But with the passage of time the animus has lessened, despite the fact that the regime is still oppressive though markedly less so, and that there has been added to the situation the particular dispute over the future of Gibraltar. Only the most ideologically committed would think of sacrificing their family holidays on the Costa Brava in order to demonstrate the strength of their anti-fascism. When it is a question of sacri-

ficing some direct personal advantage—such as the
relative cheapness of a Mediterranean holiday—the
shallowness of much of this kind of approach to
foreign affairs is fairly adequately illustrated.

The issue may of course present itself in another
way arising out of the ideological commitments of
others. British business has been under constant pressure from the Arab League to boycott Israel as the
price of continuing to operate in Arab countries. It
is a matter on which the British government has on
the whole been rather reticent, though some of its
actions would indicate a belief that Arab goodwill
and the prospects of business in Arab countries are
too important for Arab sentiment to be defied. It has
thus largely been left to individual firms to decide
where their major interests lie. This is of course yet
another example of the competitive situation in
which Britain perforce must make its living. Obviously
the major industrial countries with interests in the
Middle East could collectively defy and break a boycott of this kind; individually they are vulnerable
to it.

Quite apart from the problems that have to be
faced where foreign economic policy comes into conflict with political considerations, there is the more
general question of the role of government in further-
ing British economic interests overseas in non-political
ways. What can be done in the way of direct financial assistance is limited to some extent by international agreement. It is however felt that in other
ways British government departments and particularly
the Foreign Office could put the promotion of British
business interests higher in their list of priorities.

The importance of this aspect of British representation abroad is not nowadays often overlooked; but
to translate goodwill into action is another matter.
There have been some successful experiments in this
direction such as the "British weeks" in various
foreign cities, but although the occasional splash of
interest obviously has its value, it is upon more continuous activity that business ultimately depends. In
providing up-to-date economic and political estimates
of situations upon which businessmen can rely to
make their own decisions, the Diplomatic Service is
handicapped (as in so many other of its activities) by
its unwillingness to accept the necessity for expertise,
and its habit of moving people from post to post at
intervals far too short to allow its personnel to develop
deep knowledge of, and genuine contacts in, the
country or city concerned. The obsession with the
career-structure which runs throughout the British
civil service, and obliterates proper concern for the
nature of the jobs to be done, is nowhere more apparent than in British representation abroad.

It is also probable that the climate for British business enterprise is further influenced by the general
esteem or lack of it in which Britain is held, and that
this is affected by what is sometimes called the pro-
jection of Britain abroad. Unless people generally
think of Britain as a country of high technical achievement and productive capacity they will probably not
turn to Britain as a source of goods or technical knowledge. Despite what is sometimes thought, the British
are no tyros at propaganda—as the wartime record
of the BBC is perhaps enough to show; but they do
not much like it, and are often thankful to have the

excuse to economize on it. We almost certainly under-value certain kinds of what could broadly be termed cultural propaganda—acting as host to international congresses, sending important delegations to congresses abroad, giving recognition through official hospitality to delegations that do go. We also tend to be uncertain about the images we are trying to create and about the areas of maximum importance to us.

The reason for this uncertainty lies partly in the difficulty that is found in settling the objectives of the instruments we use for this purpose. For the BBC this has not been the case on the whole. It is recognized that its value lies mainly in the reputation which it acquired, largely during the war, of reliability where news is concerned, and of being able adequately to represent British points of view, rather than the British point of view. The difficulties of the BBC are primarily financial, resulting from the mistaken belief in the Treasury that services can be built up and audiences acquired in a hurry and a consequent unwillingness to think forward.

With the British Council the situation is different. Its "independence" of Government, which is a fiction, has been justified by claiming that its work is "non-political"; which is not the case. The presentation of the British image is a political act, and would otherwise hardly justify the expenditure of public money. The Council's accent on the "cultural" aspects of Britain's contribution to the world does not mean that no general principles are needed, either to decide what activities are most worth pursuing, or in what countries the work the British Council can do is likely to bring the greatest returns. Because of the hangover of the Commonwealth ideology we have been more concerned with the teaching of English as a form of technical assistance to ex-colonial territories than with making an impression on wealthier countries where the economic opportunities may be larger. The teaching of English has its uses, and its success helps to explain the impressive export achievements of the publishing industry; but its results accrue equally to the benefit of our American competitors. And there are other equally important ways in which a consciousness of Britain's modern role could be disseminated.

Economic objectives may of course conflict with each other. Tourism has become a factor of importance in the British balance of payments, and tourism, we perhaps rightly believe, is best encouraged by emphasizing what Britain has to offer that is unique to itself—mainly the material legacy of its past. But people who think of Britain as a country of thatched cottages and beefeaters will hardly take it seriously as an economic partner. There was something to Mussolini's objection to having Italy thought of as merely one large museum for the rest of the world to explore —even though his alternative vision proved a disastrous one.

The errors in policy are in part the results of faults in organization. The information services, the BBC the British Council, instead of being co-ordinated into a single arm of foreign policy, and judged by their respective contributions to British prestige abroad, are kept in separate compartments and in an often semi-competitive relationship. Now that we have decided to treat the whole of external relations from the geo-

graphical point of view as a single enterprise it is time
to consider functional unification as well.

One is here assuming that the general framework
of policy will remain unchanged, but there are of
course, more ambitious tasks in the economic field
which government might choose to take up. If we
accept the view that Britain (like other western European countries) cannot afford to let all its advanced
industries be taken over by American firms, and thus
accept a satellite or quasi-colonial position industrially
and intellectually—and the "brain-drain" is evidence
that this is already happening—it may be necessary
to accept the argument put forward in M. Jean-
Jacques Servan-Schreiber's now celebrated book *The
American Challenge* that this can only be done by
western Europe, including Britain, acting as a single
unit. Our own market may indeed be too small to
sustain a computer industry of our own. The talk
that has gone on about a technological community
suggests a general acceptance of this argument, and
the various attempts that have been made—usually
on a bilateral basis—at joint enterprises with other
European countries in the industrial field might be
regarded as pioneer efforts in this direction. But if
M. Servan-Schreiber is correct in assuming that the
limitations placed by national governments on their
commitment to such enterprises makes it almost certain they will fail, we are then led to his own conclusion that only a real merger of sovereignty in some
fields, leading to the creation of enterprises that could
wholly ignore national barriers, could meet the need.
The implications of a step of this kind—both inter-
nationally and in respect of its impact upon Britain's

society—are so far-reaching that they completely overshadow the much more limited issue of joining the existing Common Market, which is little more than a customs union with by now no real prospects of development into full economic integration on the United States or Soviet model. To set our sights on this broader objective would be to foreclose many other possible avenues of advance, and the question must not be considered too exclusively in economic terms. It has been raised at this stage in the argument in order to show how big can be the issues raised even by a purely economic approach.

One reason why this kind of thinking has made only limited headway in this country is that the ideal of a new "post-industrial" society, advanced by some American social thinkers like Herman Kahn and Zbigniew Brzezinski has not yet completely conquered people's imaginations here; indeed many of the young would appear to find a science-based civilization somewhat repellent because of the degree of bureaucratic centralization and depersonalization which they feel must accompany it. British scepticism has been reinforced by American failures to handle the problems of Viet Nam, of racial conflict, and above all of poverty; it is hard to take seriously a policy based upon the conviction of an imminent approach of a materialist millennium when material deprivation is so widespread, and discontent, even expressing itself in violence, so common even among the non-deprived.

But those who do not respond to the idea of Americanizing Europe and Britain voluntarily to save ourselves from being Americanized involuntarily by the mere expansive forces of the American economy, are usually equally indifferent to the preservation of the traditional and hierarchical aspects of British life. If in reaction against the natural sciences and the technological universe there were in progress a re-birth of the humanities, the pretension of playing the Greeks to the new Romans might be better-founded. But this is not the case. Our young people retreat not from science to the humanities but from the real sciences to the pseudo-sciences, sociology, social psychology, behavioural politics and so on, which are no less American in their provenance than the technology from which they are rebelling.

It may be said that such general reflections have little to do with foreign policy; but this is not so. Foreign policy is not merely an expression of the community's needs in physical security or material goods, it is also one of the expressions of its collective desires concerning the shape of the world and the nature of human society. In much more than a narrowly party sense, it is always deeply ideological. It was possible in Palmerston's England to argue that countries with liberal institutions were more likely than traditional absolutisms to provide British industry with markets or that free trade could be shown to be directly advantageous to the British economy. But as we look back upon that age, we can see that this was not the whole story. There was in those days a real belief in the validity of liberal institutions, arising out of the fact that Britain had been the leader of Europe in establishing them; there was a real connection in people's minds between the unhindered movement of commerce and the spread of more peaceful habits. An element of rationalization and even hypocrisy no doubt entered into the formulation of foreign policy, but its roots were in a commitment to one kind of society and in a wish that it should prevail universally. Perhaps this is an attitude only possible for a Great Power, and when we see very much the same kind of combination of idealism and self-interest in the case of the present-day United States we are apt to be critical of it. But even a middle-rank power cannot live wholly on a diet of limited aims.

It is thus not unreasonable to advance the hypothesis (which must later on be examined in more detail in relation to the groups and parties that make up the British political community) that the reason for the incoherence and uncertainty of British foreign policy is due, in part at any rate, to the uncertainties and confusions of Britain's own domestic outlook. Twenty-five years ago, when victory in the war seemed a reasonable expectation, no such confusion was apparent. It seemed fairly obvious that Britain would face the post-war world with a new mission, that of showing that it was possible to add to the benefits to the individual of traditional British liberalism the additional benefits of a more secure and more just social system; that to political rights could be added the right to work, the right to a decent standard of living, greater educational and cultural opportunities, and so forth. Post-war Britain was to be the Britain of the welfare-state.

We need not catalogue to what extent these objectives have been realized—and to what extent we have fallen short of them; but we can note the two ways in which this ideal affected foreign policy and was affected by it. If a liberal welfare-state was to be the frame of reference of British foreign policy, partners would instinctively be sought among countries who seemed to share the same ideals; and these were not easy to locate. North America, despite the wartime partnership and the dependence upon it that developed from 1947 onwards, was ruled out by its seeming commitment to undiluted capitalism. Hopes that had been placed in the Soviet Union—"left speaks to left"—were rapidly dissipated except in some limited though not unimportant circles—both by the international conduct of the Soviet Union, and by the revelations of the extent and depth of the Stalinist tyranny, the degree to which welfare and humanitarian considerations were subordinate elements in the communist world view. Finally, and perhaps mistakenly, the existence of similar ideals in much of Western Europe was overlooked because they found expression in a different language and were carried into effect through different institutions. The later turning towards the newly independent countries of the Commonwealth was a counsel of despair, and did not long survive except among incorrigible utopians. One was left with only a few small and scattered countries with whom some form of basic philosophical agreement appeared to exist, and there seemed thus to be no way in which the welfare-state ideal could be translated into a guide to foreign policy, not even at the United Nations.

The other way in which internal and external policy interacted is one to which we have already called attention in a different context. The expansion and development of the welfare State had been unconsciously predicated upon certain economic assumptions which were partly justified in the event. It was not fully grasped that the resources necessary to build the newer and juster society would have to be earned by a country suddenly much reduced in its capacity to command the course of the world's economy; that paying for the war and liquidating an empire would not leave much over for the creation of new wealth, and that it might be difficult enough to keep the ship afloat at all without any thought of record-breaking achievements in addition. The disjunction between social and economic policy and between domestic and external policy, which marked much of the thinking of the inter-war years upon which the wartime plans and post-war actions of government were based, is something to which historians have so far given inadequate attention. But it has been a cardinal factor in our discontents.

Even more intangible than the national mood is the element of personality in politics. One has only to look at France to see how false is the view that men don't matter and that only the collectivity counts. The British mind has been confused and bewildered about Britain's role in the world by the weakness of the country's political leadership since the war, just as foreigners have been baffled by the often blatant amateurism and narrowness of outlook of British foreign secretaries; there have been too many of them in too short a time, and for the most part they have not lived up to their difficult tasks. If M. Couve de Murville held office longer than any French minister for foreign affairs since Vergennes and was also the most successful minister since Talleyrand, this was not due either to the soundness of French policy (about which one might have reasonable doubts) or to his own virtues as a diplomat, but at least in large part to the weakness of the diplomatic opposition with which he had to contend.

One suspects however that the damage done by the inadequacy of the way in which the British case has been represented abroad—and our tolerance of idiosyncrasies in this direction has been very wide—has been less important than the failure to make policy clear at home. Why Britain should have run out of political talent at this juncture in her fortunes, or have failed to make proper use of the talent she has had at her disposal, are historical questions again. The facts cannot seriously be disputed, and this is why this inquiry into British foreign policy will inevitably conclude with some investigation of the functioning of the institutions responsible for its making and execution.

3

The Economic Preconditions

IT IS obvious enough that economic strength is an essential element in the success of any foreign policy. Upon it depends the maintenance of military power and all the other, non-coercive, instruments for affecting the course of events abroad. Economic weakness, on the other hand, can result in undue dependence upon foreign countries or international institutions for the support of the currency, and hence for the ability to buy abroad; and such dependence may be reflected in the general foreign policy field.

What is not always so obvious is the nature of economic strength which cannot be equated directly with relative prosperity or the lack of it. Most people would agree that Britain's economic position has been weak throughout the post-war period during which her currency has been twice devalued; on the other hand, for a very large section—indeed a considerable majority—of the British people, times have never been so good. Two reasons are usually given for this seeming paradox, though the importance attached to them differs usually according to the political allegiance of the speaker. It is held that through a mistaken desire to retain a more conspicuous role in world politics than her strength would entitle her to, Britain has maintained a far-flung military presence which has placed too heavy a burden on her balance of payments. As we shall see this situation is in process of being liquidated, though not fast enough for some. The second reason given is that for a country in Britain's position any growth in the economy produces an inevitable strain because of the import component of most manufactures in a country not well-endowed with raw materials, and also because of the tendency (faciliated by the growth of consumer credit) to spend always rather more than the country actually earns. And this has a dual impact on the economy since part of the spending will be on imported consumer goods, and since even where it is directed towards home products it has an inflationary effect, reflected in rising British prices and a consequent loss of export markets. Indeed, even where prices would be competitive, a very vigorous home demand may tend to discourage manufacturers from facing the greater effort and inevitable uncertainties of selling abroad.

It would be outside the scope of this essay to discuss the broader questions of economic management involved in this situation, and summed up in the familiar phrase: "stop—go". But the management of an economy so heavily dependent upon foreign trade, investment, shipping and financial services, is bound to have direct repercussions upon foreign policy, and to be affected itself by what governments do or fail to do in relation to other countries.

The importance attached by successive governments to the maintenance of London as a financial centre, and to the practice of certain countries, mainly in the Commonwealth, of keeping their reserves in London, in sterling, has had a direct effect on our relations with them. Our relations with the United States would not be the same if the Americans had not been interested in the maintenance of a world of convertible and stable currencies, and willing to act as a prop of sterling in particular. The vulnerability of Britain's currency to external pressures, partly because of London's particular role in the world's money markets, has been used as an argument against admitting

Britain to the Common Market; the Basle agreement of 8 September 1968 may have spelled the end of sterling's traditional role but it is too early to gauge the results.

Some of the cuts imposed upon government expenditure or other transfer payments in a period of restraint may have foreign policy implications, direct or indirect, quite apart from cuts in military expenditure. A good example of the latter is the restriction reimposed by the present Government on the expenditure of British tourists abroad. It is an open secret that this restriction makes no serious contribution to the balance of payments problem. It was imposed as part of the package deal designed to mollify the left-wing of the Government's supporters who believe (despite all the evidence to the contrary) that foreign travel is a luxury of the idle rich, and can therefore legitimately be curtailed in the national interest. It is also an open secret that the rich and even the moderately well-off are unlikely to be so poorly connected abroad, or to have so few business reasons for travel, as to be seriously affected by the restrictions. The people who are affected are ordinary law-abiding citizens who spend their holidays abroad counting their pennies, and give the British the reputation of being either the meanest skinflints in the world, or else of belonging to a country so close to bankruptcy that it need hardly be taken seriously.

The same effect is achieved more directly by cutting down on representational services abroad—including the British Council—or by housing British institutions in a way unbecoming to the nation's dignity. The long saga of Sir Basil Spence's never-built embassy in Rome is a good enough example. For a commercial country, we show a sublime indifference to shop-windows.

Cuts in expenditure may also be used as an excuse for minor shifts in foreign policy. The BBC over-seas services provide a good example. It is hard to be-lieve that the recent abolition of the Hebrew service, a small but rather flourishing affair, was not chalked up as another little victory for the Foreign Office's persistent pro-Arab lobby.

The principal link between economics and foreign policy is, however, in the field of trade and invest-ment. Until 1914, British policy in this respect was largely the negative one of trying to remove obstacles to British trade, and of seeing that no discrimination was exercised against British traders or investors. The general domination of a laisser faire outlook severely restricted both the help which the Government was prepared to offer traders and investors, and the num-ber of areas in which British enterprise was actively encouraged for political or strategic reasons. But the growth of protectionism generally was already forc-ing Britain into some more positive action by the time of the First World War, and still more after it and during the Great Depression. It then became a ques-tion for Britain, as for other countries, to consider whether specific and preferential arrangements could not improve the country's economic position by guar-anteeing export markets or lowering the price of necessary imports. The general acceptance after 1939 of the view that economic diplomacy of this kind and its consequences had been a source of instability and even, in part, a cause of the new world conflict, brought about strong reaction in the other direction, led by the United States, and looking to a world in which the course of trade would follow "natural" channels. The only exceptions made were on strictly political grounds such as the American encouragement of the Common Market which, being intended from the first as a full customs union, did not come under the prohibition of the GATT in which the American demands had largely been codified.

British trade in the post-war period was thus subjected to the influence of three rival concepts— Britain's own existing preferential ties with the Commonwealth; the regional system being built up in Europe from which exclusion could be harmful; and the universalist non-preferential low-tariff aspects of the GATT. British trade patterns reflect both the changes in the economy itself, and in the relevant technologies, and the impact of arrangements made or abandoned under the influence of one or other of these three approaches and their associated institutions.

The Commonwealth preferences which began with the granting by the Dominions of preferential treatment to British manufactures at the end of the nineteenth century did not become the basis of a general trading system until the 1932 Ottawa Conference. After this date both the rates of preference and the volume of trade affected reached their highest level. In 1929 only 7% of UK imports from the Commonwealth enjoyed preferential treatment and the average rate of preference allowed to UK exports to the Commonwealth was 35-36%; the figures for 1937 were 60-61% and 56% respectively.

Nevertheless it remained true as before that the Commonwealth was primarily a political association, and that it was the political factor which had helped to promote trading relations between Britain and the other members, and British investment in their economies. It was similarly the political factor which had led the countries of the Commonwealth to seek each other's support at a time of general economic contraction. The benefits of preference were not distributed as part of a general plan, but according to the pressures playing upon the negotiators. There was no consistency between commodities or countries, nor any demonstrable connection between the giving of a preference by Britain and her share in the relevant Commonwealth market, nor between the preferences she gave and the imports she actually received. There seemed little reason to suppose therefore that the system would survive intact, still less be extended in a period of economic expansion, unless fortified by a new political impetus which has in fact been lacking.

When the war ended and normal trade began again, Commonwealth preference entered a period of decline. In 1948, the percentage of British exports to Commonwealth countries enjoying preferences had dropped to 55%; by 1957, the average margin of preference available to Commonwealth goods entering Britain was only 6%. Resistance to the erosion of the system was uneven. Canada was increasingly drawn into the United States economic orbit and relatively indifferent to the preferential system; Australia and, above all, New Zealand were still vitally interested when the talks on Britain's first application to enter the Common Market began in 1961.

One factor in the relative decline of the importance of Commonwealth preference was the GATT itself, to which Britain, like most of the highly industralized countries, was an early adherent. In the main, the less developed countries and those dependent upon the production of foodstuffs and raw materials were slower to join since they were concerned with securing particular outlets for their staples rather than with increasing the general flow of goods. Australia only joined in the early days because she was afraid of being left out in any future bargaining. Nevertheless there was a steady accretion of membership from the 23 original members in 1947 to 66 members in May 1965 with a number of other countries actively co-operating in its work. From the point of view of the Commonwealth preferences the principle was the toleration of existing ones but no additions. With the reduction in the general level of tariffs that has been the main objective of the GATT, the importance of the margins of Commonwealth preference has declined, and with it their effect upon the flow of trade.

There were of course other and more powerful reasons for the relative decline in the importance of Commonwealth trade after 1952. At that date the Commonwealth whose trading position had been powerfully affected by the general dollar shortage, took something like half of Britain's exports and provided something like half of her imports, as compared with the pre-war position when the Commonwealth took about 45% of British exports and provided 37% of her imports. One reason for the decline was the increasing industrialization of the main Commonwealth countries, Australia following in the footsteps of Canada. Another was the fall in Britain's own industrial performance in the late 1950s. Britain's inability to absorb as much Commonwealth produce as Commonwealth countries needed to export was compensated for from their point of view by openings elsewhere and by the general boom conditions; had this been otherwise, it is likely that there would have been renewed pressure for increased preferences.

The decline in Britain's share of world trade was continuous from the early '50s. Between 1951 and 1959 her share in world exports of manufactures went down from 22% to 17.7%, and further to 13% in 1965-6. The proportion of trade done with the Commonwealth also decreased and was particularly affected by the decision at the Commonwealth Conference at Montreal in 1958 to dismantle controls over dollar imports. In 1957 the total of British imports was £4042 million and in 1966, £5954 million; during the same period, imports from Commonwealth countries also increased but only from £1457 million to £1606 million. Proportionately this represented a decrease from 36% to 28.6%. British exports increased in total between 1957 and 1966 from £3420 million to £5236 million, and those to the Commonwealth from £1296 million to £1310 million, representing a proportionate drop from 37.3% to 24.5%.

The decline can be traced in respect of individual countries as well. By 1964, for instance, Britain was providing only slightly over one quarter of Australia's total imports compared with almost half ten years previously, the main beneficiaries being the United States and Japan. At the same time, Britain was taking a smaller proportion of Australia's exports.

In 1959-60, Britain was replaced by Japan as the principal destination for Australian wool, and by the United States for Australian beef. In 1965-6, Japan replaced Britain for the first time as Australia's chief market. Even New Zealand was affected; before the war Britain took 80% of her exports, after the war about 65%, and Britain's share of the New Zealand market declined correspondingly.

Australia is the most striking example of the loss of Commonwealth markets, but many others exist elsewhere. In Canada's case, the changeover had come (as we have said) even earlier, and had been visible even before the war when Britain, while taking 40% of Canada's exports, only supplied 18% of her imports, with the United States of course supplying the bulk of the remainder. By 1950, the British share had fallen to 15% and by 1966 to 2·3%. India with a permanent deficit in foreign currency, and forced by endemic famine to purchase American grain, has bought more from the United States than from Britain every year since 1950 except for 1958 and 1959.

By contrast the important partners for Britain have increasingly been found in Europe. Exports to the Common Market countries increased by 14·7% of the 1957 total to 19% in 1966, and to the EFTA countries from 10% to 13%. Imports followed much the same pattern. In respect of the opportunities for British exports the pattern by the second half of the sixties was thus that while the Commonwealth took less than a quarter, Europe took more than a third. EFTA alone supplied almost as much to Britain as did the United States, and took appreciably more of Britain's exports.

It was thus not surprising that in the 1960s the most important aspect of economic foreign policy for Britain was to make certain that the expanding markets of Western Europe remained open to her, and that neither she nor her EFTA partners suffered undue handicaps from the completion in 1968 of the customs union of the Common Market countries.

It was ironical that the only exception to the general pattern was that provided by South Africa which had excluded itself from the Commonwealth in 1961, but whose trade with Britain went on growing. By 1966, South Africa supplied more to Britain than New Zealand and almost as much as Australia. As a market for British goods, she was almost the equivalent of Australia, more important than Canada and almost twice as important as New Zealand. And these considerations can again be traced in the foreign policy of the period.

The advocates for a pro-Soviet orientation of British policy got little encouragement from the trade figures. Imports from the USSR grew slowly during the period, and by 1966 were a little ahead of those from India but far below those from Australia or New Zealand. As a market for British goods, the Soviet Union did not expand in absolute terms and consequently declined considerably in relative terms between 1957 and 1966. In 1966, the Soviet Union took about half what India did and slightly less than Pakistan. Nor with the relaxation of political controls on exports to the Soviet Union can this be explained in terms of discrimination. It is obvious that the Communist countries remain an exception to the general expectation that a high level of industrialization will promote a high level of international trade. International trade is used only to fill gaps which cannot otherwise be supplied and preference is given to countries where political influence can ensure the most favourable terms. Such share as Britain can hope to get of Soviet or other Communist trade will depend on how she stands in competition with other suppliers. Politics comes in only when, as in the Cuban case, she does not feel bound by the inhibitions felt by, or imposed upon, other potential suppliers.

In the past investment abroad has been almost as important as trade in its impact upon foreign policy; though here again direct government intervention was unusual except in cases where political or strategic interests were directly involved, as for example in Persian oil. Elsewhere capital was allowed to find its own profitable outlets, whether inside the Commonwealth or outside it as in Latin America. Dividends from such investments have always been an important element in righting the balance of payments.

A particular crisis may call for the liquidation of capital assets of this kind in order to meet an overwhelming national requirement for foreign exchange and this happened in both world wars; thus Britain no longer holds such important examples of British overseas enterprise as Latin American railroads. But in favourable circumstances the tendency has been to re-invest overseas particularly in areas where rapid growth is to be expected.

Investment figures for the last decade show a quite clear pattern. From 1958 to 1960 the totals grew; they dropped in 1961–2 and were followed by another rise from 1963 onwards. Once again, the priority of Europe is the striking thing. Both the EEC and EFTA continued to receive increasing amounts of British capital even during the two years when the total invested abroad was declining.

In the Commonwealth, Canada which at the beginning of the period was the principal recipient dropped rapidly from its peak of £35·9 million in 1959 to a mere £400,000 in 1964. In 1960, it was overtaken by Australia as the major recipient. In 1958, Australia accounted for 13·1% of total British investment overseas, in 1959 for 14·4% and in 1960 for no less than 24%. After some fluctuations, it reached 29·5% in 1964.

From figures computed slightly differently from Australian sources, an even more instructive picture emerges, for they show that until 1960–1, Britain remained the principal supplier of private investment for Australia and was responsible for over half the total inflow of capital. In 1961–2, she was overtaken by the United States. And Australia's mineral and manufacturing boom since then has largely been financed by American investment. Of course one must not underestimate the continued importance of the British factor. In the whole twenty year period, 1947–67, Britain's investments in Australia came to about £1250 million—just over half the total invested there. And in recent years this has been accompanied by substantial immigration from Britain, now running at over 100,000 a year. Nevertheless, it looks as though economic ties are reinforcing those of defence and bringing Australia, like Canada before it, into membership of an American system.

Investment and migration are the fruits of individual decisions not of governmental ones which can only be of negative effect, but it would certainly look as though Britain has not been able fully to participate in the most important growth area of the Commonwealth. And some failures to grasp investment possibilities have their consequences for trade as well. The huge turnover and success of the Australian General-Motors-Holden vehicle manufacturing business largely eliminated an important market for British cars. In Europe also, the Americans have been pushing ahead with startling rapidity.

The reasons then are to be found in the same internal psychological traits that confront one whenever any area of British policy is examined. They can best be summed up in the word "defensiveness"—a tendency to react to events rather than to attempt to dominate them, both on the part of business and on the part of government. Co-operation between them, always a weak point even at the height of Britain's economic prowess overseas, was less effective than in some other countries; and the advent of a Socialist government in 1964 has merely reinforced the dominant anti-business trend in British politics.

Such assessments as have been made of British and American investment abroad show that the motives of the two countries were different. Britain's was defensive and centred on local manufacture to retain existing export markets in the face of tariff or quota barriers. The Americans on the other hand calculated their overseas investment programmes on the basis that cheaper labour and overheads would cancel out the only slightly higher costs of raw materials, an essentially optimistic, aggressive and forward-looking view. And this was true above all of Europe, where Britain's record looks most impressive. If Britain had faced the likely economic consequences of the movement for European unity while the situation was still malleable, that is to say up till 1955, she would have had a dominant share in making the eventual arrangements. By postponing serious negotiations until it was clear that her main motive for wishing to join was fear of what would happen if she were left out, she placed herself in a bargaining position whose weakness has been amply illustrated.

One could indeed argue the case for the second de Gaulle veto having been a blessing in disguise. The inevitable rise in food prices which would be the consequence of accepting the agricultural policies of the EEC (however balanced by cuts in taxation) would clearly not be reconcilable with even the present degree of income restraint, and would thus have been more than enough to tip the balance against the Government's principal strategy for improving the country's export performance. As things now stand, there is the opportunity so to improve the country's internal performance as to permit initiatives from a position of strength, and to make it possible for Britain to retain the flexibility that is essential to so varied and complex an economy. It is important of course to refuse short-term substitutes for policy such as the renewed liquidation of overseas assets which would mean accepting the kind of controlled autarkic system for which socialists hanker, but which for a commercial country spells impoverishment, human as well as material.

The question of aid to the developing countries is linked to general economic policy, and is part of the important political objective of the preservation of an ordered world. The trend of change in this branch of policy has been away from an exclusive Commonwealth orientation, and towards a more general approach to the developing countries recognizing their common interest in securing capital as well as openings for their products.

The economic background to the question can be set out in brief. British financial assistance to colonial development from government funds began in 1929, in response to the slump, and amounted then to about £1 million per annum. The Colonial Development Act of 1940 and its successors inaugurated a period of rapid growth, from an average of £16 million per annum in 1945–50 to an average of £43 million per annum in 1951–6 and of £64 million per annum in 1957-62.

Until 1957, almost no aid was given to independent countries in the Commonwealth; India, Pakistan and Ceylon thus received little or nothing except for what was channelled to them through the regional Colombo plan in 1950. In 1958, however, matters underwent a radical change, since it was appreciated that a large number of colonial territories in a very weak position economically would become independent in the near future. At the Commonwealth Trade and Economic Conference in that year the decision was made to extend aid to independent Commonwealth countries, and to associate the "old" members of the Commonwealth with Britain in contributing towards it.

The result was an important change in the scope

and amount of aid. By 1963, only a third of the aid for Commonwealth countries came from Britain; on the other hand, Britain's own contribution to aid programmes both through bilateral arrangements, and through the international institutions operating in this field, again grew rapidly. In 1959, aid through the two channels together came to £109 million, in 1961–2 to £160 million and in 1964–5 to £189 million, in 1966 to £217 million, in 1967 to £209 million —exceptionally, 1·1% of the national income.

Bilateral aid, earmarked for specific countries, which means in effect Commonwealth countries, has in recent years averaged about 85% of the total. The argument that more should be channelled multilaterally is basically a political one—that it frees Britain from the stigma of neo-colonialism, and is easier for recently independent regimes to accept. On the other hand, it is arguable that it is economically a less efficient use of funds, as it is harder to make certain that the maximum proportion is put to good use, and the minimum siphoned off into the pockets of local politicians, their families and friends. Furthermore it is probable that bilateral assistance, or the technical assistance made available through a largely Commonwealth organization like the Colombo Plan, is more economically administered than that which comes via the World Bank or other United Nations Agencies. International agencies in the contemporary world are normally staffed and administered on the very elaborate and expensive American pattern, which is quite unsuited to work in developing countries. On the other hand, international agencies are more likely to be in a position to support very large-scale projects which may in some circumstances be the most economical form of aid. The balance is difficult to strike.

One further point might be added. It is becoming increasingly obvious that in many parts of the world no aid can be effective unless it is given as part of a planned population policy. Indeed one could almost go so far as to say that assistance with family-planning should have complete priority. Britain, being a country in which the political influence of the Roman Catholic Church is relatively limited, can afford to be more definite about this than many other countries, and than the United Nations itself, where the Vatican has a bigger bloc vote than the Kremlin and has been no more chary of using it.

The most directly economic aspect of the question from the point of view of Britain is the total that ought to be given. Britain has only once reached the one per cent of GNP laid down by the United Nations as a target, though she is well towards the top of the table of givers. Except where aid is tied, which it cannot always profitably be, it is a burden on the balance of payments in the same way as are military forces stationed abroad. The justification for both can only be discussed in political terms.

What one must add from the economic point of view is the familiar caution that the terms of trade are more important than aid itself to most developing countries; it is their earning capacity that needs to be increased and in respect increasingly of manufactures as well as of primary products, and to this, the contribution of the British market is limited by its size. This applies to countries that are not normally included in the "developing" bracket. The problem which New Zealand faces in disposing of her produce must largely be met by an expansion of her sales to Japan, as Australia's has been. Similarly, African countries must continue to seek outlets in continental Europe. The flow of trade will follow the line of profitability which may often though not always be dictated by regional considerations. It means again that the patterns which reflect the era of a London-centred Empire and Commonwealth will continue to grow fainter.

The economic approach bears out the principal argument that we have been sustaining, that Britain's problems are those of a single medium-sized country, not those of an international system.

4

The Defence Policy of a Medium Power

IN A RATIONAL world, armed forces would be maintained to fulfil the needs of national security as these are defined by the makers of foreign policy. The object would be to secure the maximum protection of a country's vital interests for the minimum outlay. Even so there would of course be unsolved problems, as even the most efficient military and political intelligence would not be able accurately to predict the nature or timing of the dangers against which it was necessary to take precautions. In the real world decisions about defence policy are rarely made in this way, though they may subsequently be rationalized to suggest that they have been. The level of forces is largely fixed by what politicians believe the country can afford or will tolerate, and their composition will largely reflect traditional attitudes of groups, classes, or the entire nation, and the political and social leverage available to the different armed services themselves.

It would be fair to say that a great deal of thought has gone into defence policy since 1945, perhaps more than in any previous period except the years just before the 1914–18 war, and that a good deal has been done particularly with the central machinery for the formulation and execution of policy. Nevertheless, as one looks back over the successive changes that have been made in defence policy, it becomes clear that just as in the inter-war period the financial considerations are those that have dominated for most of the time. Our foreign policy has thus had to be adjusted to our defence policy rather than vice versa. One question is whether this process has now come to an end for the time being, and whether policy-makers can work with some conviction that the basic minimum has at last been reached. If one remains uncertain that such is the case, this is not so much because of the propensity of politicians to take the path of least resistance—which means that the armed forces will always bear the brunt of any retrenchment—but even more because of the uncertainties in the public mind about what purposes are actually served by the possession of armed forces in the modern world.

In extenuation of the confusion in the public mind certain facts need to be borne in mind. The first and most obvious—though it affects all countries and not just Britain—is the speed of technological change, which makes defence policy difficult for the layman to comprehend because, in relation particularly to weapon development, he is being asked to understand decisions that are being taken not in the light of things as they now are, but in the light of the assumed world situation of a decade hence.

Furthermore, weapons themselves have changed at both ends of the scale, and this has altered the conditions of possible or actual conflict. Public opinion has been principally concerned with the upper end of the scale, with the weapons of mass destruction. It is not true that the notion of deterrence which plays so much part in current defence thinking is a novel one; one of the uses of armies and fleets has always been to deter. What has been new is the gradual perception of the fact that the weapons of deterrence are separate from the weapons with which any likely wars would be fought. If the deterrent has to be used today, deterrence has failed; in earlier centuries it became the weapon with which the war was fought. Thus a navy confined to missile-firing submarines would not be fulfilling anything resembling the total role of navies in the past. For the super-powers, the existence of "tactical" or "battle-field" nuclear weapons has to some extent blurred this distinction; but for a power of Britain's size the actual use of tactical nuclear weapons would be tantamount to accepting the risk of almost total annihilation.

At the other end of the scale the development of small-arms, and of the techniques for handling them in guerrilla operations, or "people's revolutionary wars", has created a new dimension in warfare of which Britain has had a good deal of direct experience. It is true that colonial powers such as Britain have never had it all their own way when using armed force to bring a piece of territory under their control and to enforce their own law and order. The discrepancy of technique has never, in itself, been enough to obviate the necessity of some fighting and where, as on the old north-west frontier of India, the terrain offered problems, supplies of arms to the hostile elements were difficult to intercept, and the people were war-like, the struggle might be long-drawn out.

But modern nationalist or communist movements, with a greater sophistication of doctrine as well as weapons and with a greater propensity for risk-taking because of the ideological nature of the quarrel or the ruthlessness of their own command, have been able to disrupt to a much greater extent ordinary economic and social activities not merely in sparsely populated frontier areas but even in major cities. It could be argued in theory, as some American "hawks" would argue, that this way of looking at things is incorrect, that the real difficulty is the unwillingness of the principal western countries to use their technical superiority to the full, or to take the ruthless measures that the Communist powers would undoubtedly take in similar situations—one thinks of the position in the Soviet Union and Eastern Europe.

Nevertheless, moral and political inhibitions are as real an element in a strategic situation as any other and the fact is that guerrilla warfare in the present phase of its development is something of which defence policy has had to take notice, and of which the public may as yet be imperfectly informed despite the contributions of television.

Decolonization followed by the total withdrawal from East of Suez may be held to have made all this a thing of the past where Britain is concerned. But so long as Britain is as vulnerable to disturbances anywhere as has been argued earlier, it is not possible to be confident that this will be the case. One might however say that the use of armed force for maintaining or restoring law and order in distant countries is a task thoroughly familiar to British forces, and that the real novelty of the post-war period has not been the way in which this role has had to be faced but the commitment of British forces to a quasi-permanent role on the continent of Europe, and that it is here that foreign policy has on the whole dictated military policy rather than the other way round.

For Britain had for a long time a distinctive tradition in war and military organization which has had to be drastically revised to meet the new situation in Europe and the world. After the fifteenth century,

Britain did not endeavour to compete on equal terms with the major military powers of the continent, but used naval power and financial power to assert her interests, which were interpreted as meaning that no single power should dominate the continent, and that no hostile power should occupy the Low Countries. It was this form of barrier against over-commitment in Europe that made possible the creation of two successive overseas empires—the one that ended with American independence and its successor which has been liquidated only in our own day.

Fidelity to this tradition prevented Britain from adopting peacetime conscription as her European rivals did in the course of the nineteenth century. Although her military preparations in 1914 included a small expeditionary force in readiness for intervention in Europe, most of the army was still organized on the assumption that garrison duty overseas was its primary purpose; and the army was still considered less important than the navy as a factor in Britain's world position.

The course of the first world war forced Britain to abandon her traditional mode of operations and to mobilize her manpower for military and industrial purposes to an unexampled degree. But although Britain achieved her primary war aims, the losses she had undergone led to a repudiation of the means by which victory had been achieved. Conscription was abolished and the army, navy and new air force, recruited by voluntary enrolment and studiously professional, were again thought of in imperial rather than European terms. The most influential military thought of the period was opposed to the idea that

Britain should ever again fight a war of massed land armies. A belief in economy and the prevalence of near-pacifist sentiment in the public mind provided further impulses in the same direction. Foreign policy was for a long time conditioned by these factors.

In the end—in 1939—the compulsion of events once more changed both foreign policy and its military consequences. Britain was again forced to mobilize all her resources for war, and on an even more massive scale, though with much less eventual loss. The difference was that on this second occasion there was no rapid return to the status quo.

The development of the Soviet threat to western Europe in the course of the liquidation of the war against Germany meant that troops originally stationed in Germany to ensure the carrying out of the purposes of the victorious allies remained to safeguard the new West German state and West Berlin against being sucked into the Soviet orbit. When, following, the Korean war, the decision was taken that the West Germans should share in their own defence, British troops were required in order to reassure Germany's neighbours that the revival of German military power was no threat to them. Other aspects of the cold war and the course of decolonization also called for troops in considerable numbers for a wide variety of operations and other duties overseas. Because manpower was thus required on a scale greater than ever before in peacetime it was difficult to see how the demand could be met without continuing compulsory service.

Finally, the dissolution by the Americans of the wartime partnership in the development of nuclear weapons had the effect of making the British government decide to go ahead with the production of its own nuclear armoury—even though the tasks to be assigned to it were much harder to define in foreign policy terms than those of the conventional forces.

The classification of British forces into nuclear and conventional was however, almost as misleading for many purposes as the old classification into land, sea and air forces. The decisions that had to be made about them rested on other ways of looking at the problem.

From the financial side there were both forces of which the sole significance was budgetary, and forces which by reason of being stationed outside the United Kingdom and in particular outside the sterling area were the occasion of expenditure in foreign currencies, and so added to the balance of payments difficulties which were crucial to the country's entire economic position. And here of course the principal culprit was the British Army of the Rhine. Much of the energy of British diplomacy has been spent in trying to get the foreign exchange component of the costs of this force met by the Germans themselves, directly or indirectly, or shared among the other members of the Alliance who did not have to face similar problems, or not to the same degree. This has been a source of inter-allied friction, as the Germans refused in the new situation to go on paying what looked like the continuation of the old occupation costs.

The other principal classification of forces arises from the relationship between British armed strength and the network of alliances which itself sharply distinguished the new period in Britain's foreign policy from the traditional commitment to isolation and the free hand. No element in Britain's armoury was wholly unaffected by the existence of the alliances and notably by Britain's continued reliance upon American political, military and financial support. The troops in Africa, the Middle East and Asia could indeed be used, and were used on a number of occasions, for operations which directly affected British interests, but were held to be a matter for her alone. On the other hand, where, as in the Suez expedition of 1956, an operation of this kind was taken against the will of the United States, it could not be brought to a successful conclusion. In the case of the forces in Europe committed to the NATO commands, there was no meaningful way in which they could be used operationally, except as part of some allied effort, unless they were withdrawn for use in some other theatre or for some emergency at home. The strategic nuclear forces could in theory have been used for Britain's own purposes. But the most that could be said was that in a Great Power conflict they could be used to make certain that targets of particular interest to Britain were not passed over; and in an all-out atomic war this was a matter of decreasing interest as the scale of the envisaged destruction increased. Furthermore, for technical reasons, the very existence of Britain's nuclear weapons came to depend upon the willingness of the United States to supply vital elements in the system.

For a range of tasks of this kind it could be, and was, argued that raising forces through conscription was a wasteful method, both because of the diversion of highly trained soldiers to training duties, and because of the economic as well as military disadvantages of having to employ short-service troops for duty in distant places where travel and acclimatization further reduced the time available for their active use. The professional dislike of the system of national service was supported both by the old ideological prejudice against compulsory service, and by the view that since British security depended upon the nuclear deterrent, other forces were of symbolic rather than practical importance and could therefore afford to be small and cheap. A combination of these arguments enabled the total abolition of national service by 1962 to be announced in the white paper issued by Mr Duncan Sandys as minister of defence in 1957.

Since the early 1960s Britain has thus been once more an exception in Europe in her reliance on the voluntary system to maintain her armed forces in being, and in the run-down of her trained reserves. Originally the question was whether a society enjoying full employment could provide enough recruits by voluntary methods to reach the relatively large forces still aimed at. Since 1964 however there has been a further change with the successive cuts in force levels undertaken for budgetary reasons, and the concomitant reduction in commitments which, as a result of the two White Papers of 1968, will mean an almost complete winding up of stations outside the NATO area by the beginning of the 1970s.

The disposition of British forces is thus taking on an unprecedented form. The only considerable body of troops outside the British Isles is to be that in Germany; such naval strength as is not in home waters will principally be confined to the Mediterranean.

Any forces required by a decision to intervene in Asia, Africa or the Caribbean area and any forces allotted to the United Nations for peace-keeping duties will have to be drawn from Britain itself, or from Germany by agreement with Britain's allies.

If we suppose that these reductions will not be followed by further ones when the next economic squeeze takes place, and that we can now see the future clearly, we are still faced with important questions. The first of them still relates to the future of the voluntary system. While the Royal Air Force and Navy can perhaps continue to rely upon the value of the skills they impart to produce the necessary flow of recruits, the future of the Army is a more unknown quantity. The acquisition of skills has been stressed in recruiting, but we have also relied upon the call to adventure in serving under distant skies and different climes. "Join the Army and see the world!" It would seem to be a more appealing slogan than "Join the Army and see North-Rhine-Westphalia!" We do not yet know what the changeover will mean in recruiting, nor how far recruiting will have to depend upon extra financial inducements, which by adding to the burden on the Exchequer may create a demand for yet further reductions.

And without going into these problems there is the question of the direct impact upon foreign policy of what has already been done. How far will Britain's home-based forces be a credible factor in the eyes of friends or foes in what were areas where Britain occupied an important or even paramount position? The question is by no means a purely technical one of the mobility of forces, the capacity of airlifts, the speed at which bases can be created, taken over or re-activated; there is the much more difficult question of whether it is possible to believe that a Britain which has once extricated herself from these obligations is ever likely to persuade herself of the need to reassume them.

If less attention has been paid to this problem than it deserves, this is partly because of the very considerable efforts that have been made by British government spokesmen to conceal or minimize it. Efforts have been made to suggest that Commonwealth governments, whether directly involved like Malaysia and Singapore, or indirectly like Australia and New Zealand, have been much less disturbed by these developments than everyone in direct contact with these countries knows to be the case. The speeding-up of the timetable of withdrawal without their consent has produced an understandable scepticism about the value of British assurances, and the same holds true of the rulers of the Gulf States, and probably of Iran as well.

The temptation will be to play for safety and to make what terms are possible with whatever the main threat in a particular area is seen to be: Communist China or Nasserite Arab nationalism. In some cases such terms will not be available, and serious trouble is an ever-present possibility.

The basic mistrust which must henceforth be the lot of British policy-makers has, of course, its parallel in the grievous blows to service morale which have resulted from the manner as well as the substance of the defence cuts. It is true that the pressure from the services has been confined, in formal terms at any rate, to insisting that where forces are cut commitments must be cut also, and an equilibrium in this respect may now have been reached. But this does not of course affect the consequences for individual careers of an unexpected rate of run-down; and the attractions of the services for would-be officers cannot but have been adversely affected by the demonstration of the extent to which they are vulnerable to the exigencies of party policy.

If the relations between the services and their political masters were hammered out in the more open way which has been customary in the United States we should no doubt have heard a great deal more on these topics. What we are obliged to do is to argue not from what is said but from what is left unsaid. The most significant thing about the reduction of defence commitments overseas is that no attempt has been made to argue them in foreign policy terms, that is to say by pointing to a diminution of the threat. On the contrary, as is shown by the official attitude to the war in Viet Nam, it is still the British view that the power of China, unless balanced by forces from without the Eastern and South Eastern Asia area, will tend to dominate the scene, and be used to help subvert existing non-Communist regimes to the detriment of important western and British interests. In the case of Malaysia and Singapore no attempt has been made to argue for the view that the Indonesian territorial ambitions which led to "confrontation" are now wholly a thing of the past, and that Indonesia can be relied upon to settle down to good neighbourliness. Indeed one could not argue in this way without making nonsense of the government's expressed desires that

Australia and New Zealand should step in to take over the burden of defence that was formerly carried by Britain.

The danger to peace and stability in the Middle East which is likely to follow the final British withdrawal from the Persian Gulf is at least as difficult to discount. The threat in that area, has, however, never been as fully accepted as a fact as the Chinese or Indonesian pressure upon Malaysia and Singapore. In justifying the successive withdrawals from the Middle East, British governments have made use of the argument that Arab nationalism in its Nasserite version is substantially capable of reconciliation with British interests, and that somewhere there must exist the key to that friendship between the British and Arab peoples and their governments which only successive misunderstandings have prevented from becoming the decisive factor in the politics of the region.

A belief of this kind, deeply entrenched as it is in some quarters, and notably the Foreign Office, and dating back to as long ago as the First World War, is not easy to dislodge, even when its hollowness has been shown up by the fact that the concessions made to Arab nationalism have produced not a relaxation of pressure but rather the reverse. Nor would it be possible to assuage hostility by practising a policy of appeasement at the expense of Israel as is sometimes believed, even if British or allied opinion were prepared to go along with a policy of this kind. For although the Palestine question was undoubtedly one issue between the British government and the Arab states prior to the ending of the Mandate, the basic disharmonies in the Arab world which are at the root of the

Middle East's problems would exist even if Israel did not. On the contrary, it is Israel which in providing a common scapegoat for the Arabs' failures gives them whatever unity of purpose and action they can manage to muster. Finally, Britain's policy has not helped to solve the real human problem of the Arab refugees, no nearer solution today than in 1948.

Even with the disappearance of any Western military presence in the Arab world, the West through the oil companies, through its trading activities and even through aid programmes, maintains a different kind of presence which is also irritating in its illustration of the West's technical superiority. It is the sense of frustration on the part of the Arab intelligentsia that Nasser has been able to capture for the purpose of imposing Egyptian leadership or domination in other parts of the Arab world. It cannot be assumed that the remaining "traditional" rulers will long be immune to subversion, force or a combination of the two.

Even more serious is the fact that Nasser has allowed his pursuit of his aims at the expense both of Israel and of other Arab states to place him in a state of dependence upon the Soviet Union. The supply of arms by the Soviet Union to Egypt and other Middle Eastern states must be taken not merely as a means of communist political penetration, which some, though not all, the governments in the region may be capable of holding in check, but even more significantly in the context of Soviet naval penetration into the Mediterranean. A Soviet navy which can make use of Egyptian and Algerian bases is becoming an important factor in the strategy and politics of the area, despite the superiority in destructive power of the American Sixth Fleet. In the same way, we may expect to see Soviet naval pressure build up from the Indian Ocean into the Persian Gulf and Red Sea. Indeed, if the Suez Canal is ever reopened to traffic it is likely to be because of the additional mobility that this would give to Soviet naval strength.

While it has been stated that the British withdrawals from the Far East will permit a strengthening of British elements committed to NATO in the Mediterranean, one has the feeling that this argument was put up almost as an afterthought and that it does not represent any precise reappraisal of the military or political situation in the region. It is of course possible to take the view that over-insurance in matters of defence is as dangerous as under-insurance if the cost undermines support for national policy. The military, it is held, are prone to demand more than they really require, and it is the business of the civilian leadership to keep their requirements within bounds. But this should be done on a rational assessment of the tasks that the military may be called upon to perform, and not by the imposition of an arbitrary limit to spending, and a subsequent search for a defence and foreign policy that can be sustained within this limit.

There must always be some degree of doubt about the capacity of anyone discussing the defence aspect of policy to do so usefully without access to the information available only to government. One must hope that intelligence estimates which one does not have at one's disposal confirm the obviously more optimistic view of the future which would alone suffice to justify the present governmental stance in these matters. It is in fact impossible either to know the extent to which Britain has the resources to inform herself of the nature and extent of the threats to her security that exist, or whether she depends to any considerable extent upon her allies (and notably the United States) in the intelligence as in other fields, or whether her own assessment of the situation and that of her allies differ to any notable extent.

It is one thing to say that a defence policy, if it is not to be too expensive to bear, must be based on the "intentions" rather than the "capacities" of possibly hostile powers; it is quite another thing to be confident that the capacity for assessing intentions is an adequate one. It must always be remembered that what matters in the intelligence sphere is not simply the ability to collect by open or clandestine means the required information, or even the ability to interpret it. There is also the question of how far such intelligence is considered when policy is framed, and how much of it comes up against insuperable barriers either within the bureaucracy or at the political level when it challenges powerful preconceptions about the external environment.

The polarization of world power between the Soviet Union and the USA is relevant here, as at every stage of this discussion. The most detailed assessment, for instance, of the capabilities and intentions of Middle Eastern rulers or of parties or groups that might replace them would obviously be little use if there were to be a profound alteration in the outlook of either of the Great Powers. One can see what difference it would make to one's prognosis as the future course of the Arab-Israeli conflict if one believed that the Soviet Union would wash its hands of the Arabs, or the United States conclude that Israel was expendable. It is only on the basis of certain assumptions about the likely behaviour of the super-Powers that regional planning in foreign or defence policy makes any sense.

Where the Soviet Union is concerned, there has been no more persistent illusion among the framers and critics of British policy than that which holds the "cold war" has been simply an expression of the divergent interests of the Russians and the Americans, and that British statesmen can have a credible role as mediators between them. Whatever reservations there may be about the tendency among some Americans to identify all movements to which they are opposed as communist, and to treat the communist movement itself as more monolithic than it is today, the basic element in the "cold war" remains what it has been ever since the gap between Soviet Russia and the non-Soviet world first opened up as a consequence of the Russian Revolution and its immediate aftermath.

Whatever minor modifications the Russians have made at home in the management and control of their own society, they have not shifted from the fundamental belief that Moscow-led communism is the only permissible pattern of development not merely for their own society but for the rest of the world as well. The Russians recognize the obstacles that have been placed in the way of assisting its expansion by force of their area of control; they may even be prepared through disarmament and arms control agreements to rule out certain forms of competition with their

American rivals, but these developments in no way imply a modification of the central tenets of their own creed. To do them justice, they at no point have pretended otherwise. If people in Britain or elsewhere misinterpret tactical changes and profess to believe in the possible "liberalization" of the Soviet Communist system, in some kind of "convergence" between Russia and the West, or in an open-ended detente, they have only themselves to blame when they find they have been deceived. Indeed it is rather the other way round. As dissatisfaction with communist dogmatism and its results has developed in Eastern Europe and has been echoed however discreetly in the Soviet Union itself, the reaction of the Soviet leadership has, predictably been to tighten rather than loosen its hold. It has become increasingly aware of the fact that its strategic dispositions in Europe have been based upon the fidelity of regimes which in most instances owe their survival as well as their inauguration to Soviet military power, and would now disappear for good if that power were to remove itself or be neutralized. It is probable that communism as such has by now struck deeper roots in the Soviet Union where it has been implanted for fifty years than in the rest of eastern Europe where it has been in power for less than half that time. But even in the Soviet Union critical and centrifugal forces obviously exist. What is conclusive, for the present wielders of political power in the Soviet Union, is that a liberalized communism whatever shape it might ultimately take would have no use for them. It is a correct presumption of Marxist historiography that ruling classes and groups do not normally surrender their power without a struggle; there is no reason to make an exception for the Soviet Union or its henchmen in East Germany, Poland and elsewhere.

The acceptance by the West of a policy of non-interference in Soviet dominated eastern Europe, an acceptance illuminated by the Czech crisis of 1968, does not mean that events there are irrelevant to the foreign policy of the western countries. If for no other reason, the fortunes of the two halves of Europe are linked together by the German and Berlin questions. So long as the Soviet government is determined to uphold the East German regime in an uncompromising form and to back up its harassments against Berlin, progress towards the normalization of relations in central Europe is impossible. By making any rapprochement between Western Germany and Eastern Europe more difficult and by doing its best to destroy confidence in the peaceful intentions of the West German government, the Soviet Union is contributing to bringing about the growth of precisely those nationalist and revisionist elements in West Germany that it most professes to fear.

The denunciations of West Germany are only a facet, furthemore, of the general and persistent efforts of Soviet diplomacy to undermine and destroy the solidarity of the Atlantic alliance system and its members' confidence in each other. Where western Europe is concerned it has been possible to make out a case for this activity being mainly of a defensive kind; unable seriously to challenge the American guarantee of western Europe, the Soviet Union has had little expectation of being able forcibly to alter the situation to its advantage.

So long as the economic evolution of western Europe continues at a satisfactory pace, and so long as the allegiance of the French and Italian working classes to the Communist Party depends upon its remaining virtually a party of the status quo, no great harm can come of the attempts to weaken western solidarity—even the detachment of France from its allies is more a matter of the French getting their American guarantee at a cut rate than of a serious reversal of French policy. But if there were an economic setback of major dimensions, if the strikes and student disorders in France in the summer of 1968 heralded a new period of internal instability in one or more of the larger western European countries, if governments became dependent upon communist support for their survival, the grounds for optimism would largely disappear. There is no reason in the nature of things why the Soviet government should not draw what profit it could from such a situation, always provided that it did not involve a head-on clash with the United States.

Outside Europe, where the American involvement is more speculative and where methods other than the all-out application of military strength have greater prospects for success, one must assume that the Soviet Union will be driven both by the logic of it own position and by its competition with China inside the communist movement to go on probing for points of weakness and to insert its controlling influence whereever possible. The disappointments the Russians have had to face in both Africa and Latin America should not be interpreted to mean their readiness to abandon the struggle. And, as has already been seen, the areas where Soviet prospects seem at their brightest are the Mediterranean and the Arab Middle East where British interests are directly engaged. Nor can one assume that the Arab countries alone are of direct interest to the Soviet Union in this connection. Attempts to win Iran away from its close links with the West, whether through diplomacy or the encouragement of communist or pro-communist forces, will no doubt continue.

Of even greater ultimate significance to Britain is the likely evolution of Soviet policy in the Indian sub-continent. Until very recently one result of the Sino-Soviet dispute had been to tighten the links between the Soviet Union and India; India has received assistance from both the West and the Soviet Union and has pursued a foreign policy on the whole congenial to the Russians. Pakistan has been in the curious position of being part of the anti-Communist western defence system through CENTO (the Central Treaty Organization) while preserving good relations with Communist China arising from their common hostility to India. It now looks as though the Soviet Union is trying to repair its relations with Pakistan even at the cost of incurring Indian hostility. Taken together with the obvious intention of the Soviet Union to become a naval power in the Indian Ocean, these developments must call for some reassessment of western policy in general and British policy in particular.

Nothing has been more striking about the consequences of Britain's retreat from empire than the relative neglect by British opinion of the affairs of the Indian sub-continent by comparison with those of Africa. For the Indo-Pakistan conflict over Kashmir

—a piece of unfinished business created by the manner of the British withdrawal—has been a major factor in world politics. Britain, with important economic interests in both countries, and enjoying some measure of goodwill in both societies, has found it almost impossible to steer a course which has not offended one or other government. What could have been the principal economic and cultural link between Britain and Asia has thus been deprived of its full significance. It may well be that the depth of feelings on both sides of the Indo-Pakistani dispute is such that no solution can be found, but there could certainly be no more urgent or important task for Britain than to seek to remedy the disunity of the sub-continent. So long as it persists, both India and Pakistan are highly vulnerable to centrifugal forces within as well as to pressure from without. Only the creation of an Asian balance of power can justify the withdrawal of the West; and such a balance cannot be created while India is weak.

A plea for greater awareness of where the main dangers to stability lie is not to suggest that Britain alone can exercise more than a marginal influence except in a very few areas. What is necessary, however, is than an appreciation should exist of where Britain's principal interests lie so that within the framework of Britain's alliances, British influence can be fruitfully exerted. Military and economic dependence need not involve intellectual dependence as well. This is something which must be kept in mind when we turn to the most central of all the problems of British foreign policy, the scope and purposes of the British alliance system.

5

Permanent Partners or Unchanging Interests?

THE MOST striking difference between the foreign policies of pre-war and post-war Britain is her abandonment of the policy of isolation, better-styled perhaps the policy of the free hand, and the substitution for it of a policy of alliances. And there is no aspect of British policy for which the reasons are less well understood. Yet it should not be regarded as something peculiar, as the same is true of the United States whose tradition of non-entanglement was even older, and even more deeply rooted. The only countries to-day which can practise a policy of neutrality are those which for particular reasons are so placed that there are external factors that help to guarantee their security against infringement. The "non-aligned" countries are not neutral in the classical sense, but the exponents of a different form of political grouping which is often no less a commitment than an alliance would be.

The present vogue of alliances has three main causes. Countries cannot by themselves sustain the burden that the pursuit of security or other interests imposes upon them. The United Nations (like the League before it) has failed to provide security through the workings of an international organization. To the ordinary divergences of outlook and interest between the nations there has been added the ideological divide of the "cold war".

The importance of the last of these is that it promotes a differentiation between the old pre-1914 alliances and the contemporary ones. The alliances of the eighteenth and nineteenth centuries, entered into for mutual convenience between governments of much

the same kind, were in their very nature imper-
manent. When their benefits were exhausted, the
participating countries would seek alternative partners. But the ideological factor, particularly in a
world where power is so unevenly distributed, makes
this impossible. Although Britain's immediate post-
war alliances (the treaty of Dunkirk with France, and
the Five-Power Brussels treaty of 1948) had as their
immediate purpose the provision of guarantees as
against the renewal of a threat from a future remili-
terized Germany, they were swallowed up in the
Atlantic Treaty of 1949 which was clearly directed
towards halting the westward spread of communism
in Europe. The less effective CENTO and SEATO
(South East Asia Treaty Organization) treaties represent the nearest it has been possible to come to establishing an alliance system to deal with the threat of
communist expansion in western Asia and south-east
Asia respectively.

On the other side, the Warsaw Pact is clearly an
expression of the determination of the Soviet Union
not to permit the withdrawal of its eastern European
neighbours from the communist bloc or to experiment
with alternative patterns of socialism; it is therefore
very much more than a mere arrangement for guaran-
teeing mutual security.

While none of the treaties or organizations which
make up the pattern of Britain's alliances are immutable—and while it could be claimed that neither
CENTO nor SEATO are exactly appropriate in
the present situation of the regions they cover—it
is still true that an outright reversal of alliances is
not possible for Britain, or indeed for most other

countries on either side of the divide between the communist or non-communist worlds, since it would imply a massive shift in internal policy and ideology as well. The two sides are not symmetrical. The Soviet Union will always repress by force any attempt by her allies either to shift their alliances or go neutral; the United States would no doubt accept the freely reached decision of one of its allies to leave its security system. But the actuality is the same. The arguments of military security are—again on both sides— fortified by those of economic interdependence. And this is truer of no country than it is of Britain.

Trade with the Soviet Union and other communist countries has, as we have seen, become somewhat more important, and has prospects of growth, dependent though these are upon the evolution of the economies of the Soviet bloc. But such trade remains and will remain marginal as compared with the intricate network of commerce, credit arrangements and capital movements between the countries of the non-communist world which is the key to Britain's economy. It is out of the question that any class in Britain would voluntarily accept the degree of impoverishment which exclusion from the world system of trade and payments would involve. Nor can Britain accept with equanimity the withdrawal from that system of any further important part of the world.

For those who are disturbed by the materialism of this argument, one might add that no considerable section of British opinion would willingly accept the restrictions upon personal freedom which incorporation into the rival world system would, as experience has shown, inevitably entail. In these circumstances, to talk of leaving the Atlantic Alliance, or of recovering freedom of action in this sense, is either to give voice to an absurd if intelligible nostalgia or to indicate a willingness to see Britain become part of the Communist world. The problem is not whether Britain should remain part of a western security system, but how that system should best be organized and what degree of integration within it is acceptable. Upon these questions differences of opinion are legitimate and they are too important to be settled in any cursory fashion.

The British official view of the problem has undergone several changes since the immediately post-war period. The accent at that time was upon securing American assistance in the immediate task of rebuilding the European economy and an American guarantee for western Europe's security. The Marshall Plan and the Atlantic Alliance were the products to a considerable extent of Anglo-American co-operation, both in their inception and in their translation into the Organization for European Economic Co-operation (OEEC) and NATO.

European policy was definitely subordinated by Britain to the Anglo-American tie, and the Brussels Treaty itself was entered into only as a preliminary to seeking American support. Despite much hostile feeling in Britain towards the idea of a rearmed Germany, the American insistence that this was essential to any realistic scheme of European defence was perforce accepted by the British government; and it was typical of the British role at that time that it was a British initiative which, after France's repudiation of the European Defence Community, produced an alternative in the shape of the Western European Union

(WEU) treaty, and the commitment to keep British forces on the continent.

The priority that Britain gave to the link with the United States was acceptable to the older members of the Commonwealth—the primary dependence for defence of Canada, Australia and New Zealand was now upon the United States—but it was less acceptable to some of the newer members who deplored other aspects of American policy, and above all it was highly suspect in Europe. This was because the concentration upon the objective of making certain that the United States would not once more retreat into isolation, and the willingness to make long-term agreements dictated by this over-riding objective, was allowed to overshadow in the British mind the contemporary movement for new institutions confined to Europe. Even where Britain went along with the creation of such institutions—as in the case of the Council of Europe—she did her best to limit their powers and minimize their role. While the continental countries were intent on bringing Britain into the movement for European unity, and were prepared to offer Britain a considerable role in leading and shaping the movement—the prestige of the one major European country successfully to have avoided Nazi domination was then at its height—Britain itself was determined to reject the call. Nor can everything be blamed on the dogged insularity and wilful insensitivity of Ernest Bevin; the policy was supported as far as we know by his permanent officials, and confirmed by his successors.

The motives of the British government in refusing to be drawn into the task of "building Europe" were complex; but because they derive from attitudes that still exist, it is necessary to summarize them. It was easier to maintain aloofness from Europe than from America, because America was thought to be strong and a source of strength, and Europe weak and a source of weakness. The rapidity of Europe's recovery was unforeseen. The ideological foundations of the European movement were largely alien to British statesmen and British political parties—Christian Democracy which played so large a part in the early stages was unintelligible in a mainly protestant or secularist context. The welfare-state and British-style socialism might suffer, it was held, if economic life had to be regulated on principles laid down by international institutions dominated by other social philosophies.

More important still, the Europeans asked more than the Americans; the British commitment would be a more far-reaching one. Despite the lip service paid by the text of the Atlantic Alliance treaty to other forms of co-operation than military, the organization it had created remained primarily a security one. The economic implications of a close dependence upon the United States involved no more than adherence to the general principles of non-discrimination that the Americans were trying to get accepted as the basis of the post-war world economy. Although an acceptance of these principles was productive of short-term difficulties, and although their long-term implications spelled an end to any prospect of refurbishing or strengthening the special economic links between Britain and the countries of the Commonwealth, it was generally held that from Britain's own point of view they had much to offer. The protective and discriminatory devices which most countries had adopted as a result of the Great Depression and the philosophy of economic autarky upon which they were based were ultimately incompatible with British economic interests; and any measures that looked like preventing a recurrence of this cycle were to be applauded. Finally the restoration of British agriculture begun in the 1930s, given a tremendous impetus by wartime needs, and prolonged into the peace was not endangered by United States' policies which conceded a special place to agriculture, since it occupied a special place in the United States itself.

By contrast, the European movement seemed an open-ended one. Its methods might be economic, but its ultimate purposes were political: to end the internecine conflicts of the western European nations by merging their sovereignties in some larger unit. Instead of maintaining the maximum of national freedom of action compatible with the common pursuit of security, emphasis was laid upon the substitution of decisions reached through the operation of supranational machinery. Ultimately, the creation of a federal Europe was envisaged. Although the majority of the movement's adherents were upholders of the view that American support would continue for some time to be necessary if pressure from the East were not to cut short the construction of the new Europe, ultimate independence of the United States was envisaged as a possible and desirable goal. The United States was a model for emulation rather than a full partner in the enterprise. Britain could not fully accept, and had no inner drive to make her accept, this view of the American role; nor in the late 1940's and early 1950's, when the Commonwealth and Empire were still living entities, was Great Britain itself a very obvious candidate for participation in a purely European federal system.

A detailed study of the period would no doubt reveal alongside these broad considerations of principle other doubts and fears, based upon a narrower and more immediate calculation of where British economic self-interest lay. But the result was the same; the "Six" were allowed to build their own version of Europe on the basis of the Coal and Steel Community, the European Economic Community (Common Market) and Euratom. The creation of this system of close links between the Six without British participation removed the initiative from Britain where European policy was concerned. It now became a question of how Britain would react to the creation of such a system. The most immediate source of anxiety was economic—an important market for British goods would be rendered more difficult of access by a discriminatory tariff. American and, to the extent they were permitted, British companies, would be obliged to site new plant within the common market tariff wall with adverse consequences for employment in Britain.

The first attempt to deal with the situation was therefore also an economic one, the suggestion that an industrial free trade area might be created out of the Common Market, Britain and certain other non-participating countries which would remove the discrimination against British exports, without entailing any alterations in British agricultural policy and with no political overtones. This proposal was rejected by the

Six in January 1959, and was followed by the creation of the European Free Trade Association linking Britain, the Scandinavian countries, Switzerland and Portugal in a grouping dedicated almost exclusively to the removal of trade barriers between the member countries. Although the countries concerned were not without their own importance for Britain's trade, it was generally held that they could be no substitute for the larger and more diverse opportunities open among the Six and that EFTA was thus more of a bargaining weapon than an ultimate answer to Britain's problem.

The justice of this view was shown by the decision to apply for membership of the Common Market itself —a decision taken by the Macmillan government in 1961. The rejection of this application in 1963 did not prevent its renewal by the new Labour government which came into power in the following year. The second rejection in 1967 which was apparently un-expected by the government, although not by most close observers of the European scene, was officially met only by the reiteration of statements that the British application still stood; and adherence to the Common Market remains the policy of all three political parties. But it may well be that this apparent unwillingness to reconsider policy will prove only temporary.

Once again, Britain appears to be in a position where she has no choice but to wait on the decisions of others, and to decide how to react to them. Those who wish to adhere to the original decision are no doubt moved by the original arguments; but are these still valid, particularly on the political side?

It has been repeatedly stated in connection with Britain's second application for membership of the Common Market, that Britain accepts not merely the existing economic institutions and policies—subject to a transitional period of adaptation—but also its political objectives. But it would be idle to pretend that the Common Market today represents a step towards the kind of United States of Europe that was in the mind of its original promoters. It is not simply that France in the person of General de Gaulle has repudiated any adherence to the doctrines of supranationalism in favour of national self-assertion in its most uncompromising form, but also that relations between the countries of the Community have not taken on their expected shape.

For the first decade after the war it seemed an axiom of French policy that Britain should be drawn into any European organization in order to provide a counterweight against Germany, once that country were to recover its innately formidable strength. In the last decade, the position has been reversed; it is Britain that wants to come in and France that is keeping her out. The reason is that the French have discovered, or believe they have discovered, that their earlier fears of Germany were misplaced. The principal political object of the creators of the ECSC (European Coal and Steel Community) and the EEC has been achieved, in that the secular quarrel between France and Germany seems to have been buried for good. More than that, within the Six themselves a special Franco-German relationship, given expression in the treaty of January 1963 (the month of de Gaulle's first veto), has grown up, and has been a means through which France has exercised its hegemony within the group as a whole. No doubt there are reasons why this should be so; the German fears of a French deal with Russia at the expense of any hope of German reunification, the lingering doubts as to the permanence of the American guarantee, the Germans' own understandable self-mistrust. But whatever the reasons, the facts speak for themselves: every effort by the Germans to argue the case for British entry—for which they have good economic and political reasons—or for cushioning the impact of Britain's exclusion has run into insuperable French opposition. In the last resort the Germans have always given way. So far from the Common Market being a political community in embryo, it is simply an instrument through which France achieves its national purposes. It is not on the German government only that the French have exercised their influence; German opinion has also on these matters begun to follow the French lead, and to regard the British relationship with the United States as meaning that she belongs to an "Anglo-Saxon" world, and therefore can have no place in a united Europe until these ties are severed.

French domination of the Common Market exercised through her ability to bring it crashing down by withdrawing at any moment is patent in the evolution of the economic policies of the Six. Nor does France show any sign that she holds her obligations towards them as being any more binding than economic arrangements are in normal circumstances; the claim of the Community's organs to have a say in what she does is specifically repudiated. Just as

Britain, after Labour took power, irritated her EFTA partners by imposing an import surcharge without prior consultation with them, so France, when faced with economic difficulties after the upheavals of May-June 1968, went her own way and disputed any special right of her partners to have a say.

It may be the case that all this should be ignored, and that it should be put down solely to the immutable personal philosophy of General de Gaulle. There are two difficulties in the way of accepting this optimistic view. In the first place, the de Gaulle policies seem to be acceptable to a large enough section of the French economic and governmental élite for it to be most improbable that a successor government based on the same social and political alignments would repudiate the Gaullist heritage on this point. In the second place, in any wider reshaping of the French political scene such as might follow de Gaulle's disappearance, the forces that might come to the fore would quite probably not be those associated with the "European idea" in its original form.

The claim that Gaullism is just a detour from Europe's predestined road to unity would be comforting if correct; but the evidence is too scanty for all Britain's hopes to be pinned upon it being true.

There are also more fundamental reasons for doubting whether the arguments for "entering Europe" are as powerful today as when Whitehall and the government were first converted to them in 1960-1. The success of the "Kennedy round" suggests that free trade between the major industrial countries is now increasingly accepted by all of them as a desirable goal. If that be the case the importance of specific arrangements like the Common Market must diminish. The real obstacles to world trade seem to lie in two other directions; the inability of the less developed countries to earn enough to pay for necessary imports and service necessary investment, with the consequent growth of the gap between "rich" and "poor" or north and south; and the inadequacies of the world system of currency and credit. The Common Market countries have been doing something and may do more about the former problem, but there is no reason to believe that Britain's adherence would make much difference. In so far as the task is one of co-ordinating the policies of the advanced countries, the Organization for Economic Co-operation and Development—with its wider membership—is a more appropriate forum. On currency questions, the Six have not yet got to the stage of handling their own internal difficulties, and French dislike of any of the schemes for improving the wider international mechanisms means an unreadiness on the part of the Common Market countries to contemplate more than the rescue operations recently performed on behalf of the pound.

On the political side the doubts are even more fundamental. There has always been in the British acceptance of the basic political objectives of the European movement the underlying proviso that the institutions it developed would be democratically controlled, that is that they would embody the principle of responsibility to an elected parliament or parliaments. One of the main criticisms of the existing Communities has been the role allegedly played by "faceless bureaucrats" responsible to no one. At the time the Communities were established it did not

appear that such a proviso was unreasonable; the experience of various forms of totalitarianism in Europe
seemed to have cured most of its countries of any
leanings towards non-democratic forms. It was con-
fidently assumed that the creation of a directly elected
European Parliament would be high on the agenda of
the Communities themselves.

Even the frustration of this hope could be put down,
like so much else, to the French desire to keep the
Communities from developing further. But today
things look different. The new governments have done
much for their countries, and in terms of output the
countries of western Europe can look back to a remark-
able period of growth; but growth is not everything.
There is a social malaise, in part the product of affluence itself, in part the protest of large social categories
who have hardly shared in it. And this malaise, reflected in student and industrial unrest, is in the vital
case of Germany given a sharper edge by the continued inability of the German government to bring
about the national goal of reunification.

From the British angle, the important and sinister
element in these developments is that they have once
again called into question for many Europeans the
ability of parliamentary-style governments to deal
effectively with the needs of modern society. The de
Gaulle regime in France which already represents a
very considerable retreat from full parliamentarism—
notably in its attitudes to the mass media—has shown
that it is a fact that certain problems—in this case
above all the completion of decolonization—can only
be handled by a government not dependent upon the
shifting sands of party. And the lesson has been

learned, perhaps too well, and by Left as well as Right.

It would be a mistake to claim that Britain is immune to the new current of anti-parliamentary ideas. We have our revolting students and other exponents of direct action, and far more important, a tendency within organized labour to seek its objectives if necessary in defiance of government, even of a government which is itself an emanation of the labour movement. But compared with the position in the other principal west European countries, the parliamentary process is still much more meaningful to the average British citizen. Indeed much of the irritation that is expressed with British institutions arises from the feeling that the parliament is too weak in relation to the executive, not too strong.

The present difficulties of the democratic systems of western Europe may prove evanescent; the uncompromising attitude taken up by the Soviet Union towards any relaxation of totalitarian structures in Eastern Europe may remind those outside its clutches of the value of the freedoms they possess. France may make a peaceful transition to a non-Gaullist Republic; the German Grand Coalition may discover a capacity for positive action, and the neo-Nazi threat may recede; Italy may get out of the phase of weak minority government and find a method of forcing needed structural reforms through its legislature. But until it is clear that the more optimistic view is the better-founded one, there is bound to be some brake on British desires finally and irrevocably to merge Britain's destinies with those of such uncertain partners.

Even from the practical point of view it is difficult

to see how any kind of a federal system could be created in which the component units were not themselves broadly democratic in respect of their own institutions; indeed the Constitution of the United States expressly provides for the guarantee by the Federal Government of a republican form of government to every State. And if no federal structure is conceivable, if the only form that Community can take is that in which authority is shared between the bureaucracy of the Commission and Ministers to a large extent shielded from the operation of the democratic process, it is difficult to believe that as a political instrument it can have very much appeal in this country.

Many of the beliefs which are held in Britain about contemporary Europe, and which are used as arguments why Britain should not involve herself more deeply than necessary in its affairs, are erroneous; for instance, the common assumption that Britain is an unchallengeable leader where the social services are concerned. But the doubts about the continued political stability of many European regimes are perfectly understandable and reflect serious anxieties within the continental European countries themselves. It is this feeling more than anything that may explain the appeal which a North Atlantic Free Trade Area (NAFTA) makes in some quarters. The economic advantages as compared with membership of the Common Market are, as we have seen, hypothetical at best. What attracts is the idea that Britain would be associated in the first instance with countries whose democratic institutions she believes to be as stable as her own. In dealing with the United States, the older members of the Commonwealth, Scandinavia and

Switzerland, Britain would be dealing with countries with whose ways of doing business and with whose processes of thought she feels herself well acquainted. It is psychologically a much easier enterprise to contemplate than plunging into Europe.

So much having been said, it remains true that the NAFTA alternative is an unreal one. Its advocates have already extended the idea from that of a regional grouping to that of an open-ended free trade association for which the Common Market itself would be an eligible member. But the economic benefits could more simply be achieved through the GATT and it is most improbable that the Common Market would join such an association for the same reasons as those which led it to reject the earlier British proposals for a European Free Trade Area. We would thus get an association of which the United States was the principal member and Britain the only important European one, while Britain's most important European trading partners remained aloof and even hostile. It is not difficult to see the economic, political and psychological disadvantages of such a situation. Indeed it could be argued that Britain would gain more by becoming a State of the American union with full access to the benefits of belonging to a larger and richer human group.

Such discussions are in the realm of theory. The initiative for any kind of NAFTA would have to come not from this country but from the United States and, despite the interest shown in the idea by some prominent American figures, it seems more than unlikely that any American administration will so reverse a well-established line of policy.

While the discussion of the NAFTA alternative may be academic, it is not necessarily unprofitable. It is useful that alternative lines of policy for Britain should be canvassed, if only to show that there can be no question of the country being placed in a position where it can have no foreign policy other than waiting for the French to change their minds. It is also better that alternatives should be discussed, rather than devices for getting round the French veto and buying ourselves into Europe by offering some allegedly irresistible dowry. At one moment it was thought that this would consist in the offer of Britain's nuclear weapons to form the basis of a European deterrent. The offer had no appeal, because the French, who were the objectors, believed in national deterrents and not in a collective one. And by now, as we have seen, the whole idea of a European nuclear armoury conflicts with the basic strategy of working within a bi-polar framework for non-proliferation and eventual arms control and arms reduction. Latterly, the idea of a technological community has come to the fore; but as we have seen, while this is a desirable complement to entering a Common Market, it is meaningless until Britain enters and is in no sense a method for securing entry. And because the technological community would be based upon a European programme of advanced research, some recent actions, notably Britain's withdrawal from participation in European work on high energy physics, must suggest to possible partners that such interests are regarded as marginal when the national budget is in question.

Does the discussion of alternatives mean that no choice is possible? Must we admit that what is within reach is not desirable and that what is desirable is not within reach? Discussions on British foreign policy where not influenced by wishful thinking often give one this impression. The reason is that most definitions of British interests leads one to conclude that they point to foreign policies rather than to a foreign policy.

From the narowly economic point of view the maximum latitude is desirable so that trade and investment can be carried on wherever it appears most profitable. From the point of view of technological and industrial development, there is a need to broaden the domestic market available to British industry and its basis in research and development, and this means a fairly far-reaching commitment to Europe which could involve so great a degree of the mixing-up of economies of the various countries that only a much more developed version of the European Economic Community would suffice. In so far however as the pressure of the Communist world is likely to be maintained and to demand military guarantees to render it innocuous, no western defence system which is not based upon the strength of the United States can possibly be acceptable to Britain.

The pursuit of British interests in contemporary conditions thus points away both from Britain's traditional isolation and from the utopian universalism of the United Nations ideologies. Britain has need of permanent partners; but the partners are different according as to whether one approaches the problem from the defence or the economic-industrial angle. Nor of course are these easy to separate, given the high importance which defence orders have assumed for many aspects of industrial development. One obvious element in the anti-American accent of part of the European movement is the feeling that the United States has used its preponderance in the Alliance to secure a virtual monopoly in Europe for its own defence and aeronautical industries.

The issue is often blurred by talking of a European Community having a common foreign policy. Such a foreign policy would in fact be no different in the problems it had to face from the foreign policies of the component countries; relations with the United States, the Soviet bloc, the rest of the world. The individual members of the EEC even now have very considerable differences between themselves on many of these points. Britain's membership would add new possibilities of discord. Either such a Community would have to reject all policies which did not command general adherence and thus condemn itself to almost total passivity, or it would have to adopt a number of individual countries' policies for which various of its members were not prepared to make the necessary sacrifices. The original formation of the United States was possible because there was a single objective, independence; its perpetuation was possible because neutrality made it unnecessary for the country to have an active foreign policy. But as soon as the quarrels of Europe overspilling onto the oceans and into the New World made some kind of policy essential the unity of the country was placed in considerable jeopardy.

The failure to make greater headway either within the Atlantic Alliance or within the European Communities arises from the fact that their institutions are incapable of resolving many of the differences of policy between the member-States. These differences must be hammered out before there can be further dramatic progress on the institutional front. Britain cannot in fact enter a European federal system and surrender her autonomy in foreign policy until there is a solid agreement on the future relations between such a Europe and the United States. The Atlantic system cannot operate to greater advantage until there is agreement on the respective roles of its European and North American components on basic strategy both in defence and in negotiation.

The question is whether the present institutional structure is sufficient to promote the necessary discussions and partial agreements that would be the preliminaries for a much more far-reaching acceptance of the idea of permanent partnership than can at present be envisaged. For some purposes the necessary machinery already exists; in respect of general policy, especially in relation to developments in central and Eastern Europe, and in respect of cultural and scientific affairs, the Council of Europe; in respect of the economy, the OECD, which might properly reassume a European role as well as its present wider one; in respect of defence, Western European Union, which might perhaps usefully extend its membership to include all European members of NATO.

What has been lacking has been the will to use these different approaches to make certain that when the time arrives at which the immediate circumstances exist for a more far reaching step towards European unity to be taken, it will not be held up because of major differences of opinion as to what ought to be done afterwards. It may be that this recital of possibilities shows a lack of constructive imagination which would be typical of the nineteen sixties as compared with the two preceding decades. In particular there seems no appropriate forum for seeking a common European policy within the framework of the United Nations. Suggestions that this is something desirable have in the past run up against strong objections. It has been held that any sign that the European countries, many of them ex-imperial powers, were getting together would inflame the suspicions of the Third World and look like a conspiracy of the rich and powerful against the poor. Such arguments have played a particularly prominent part in British discussions of this question. At an earlier period there were some indications that Britain might better forward her purposes in the United Nations by developing informal ties with other Commonwealth countries represented there: but the openness of some of them, notably India, to Soviet pressure makes them wholly unreliable even on the moral and verbal plane. The non-Communist European countries are the only group in the United Nations who do not act as one, although their interests are often a target for others.

The United Nations is likely to continue in being. There are many issues of the contemporary world—of which disarmament is the most important—for which it is almost the only conceivable framework. When the ties between metropolitan countries and their former overseas possessions weaken, as they will, the specialized agencies are likely to take on a more important role in dealing with the non-political aspects of world tensions than they do at present. Finally, on the political side, the threat to law and order in so many parts of the world suggests that the interposition of United Nations peace-keeping or inspection elements is likely to be more rather than less frequently demanded. It seems hard to believe that a group of the most advanced of the member-States have nothing of their own to contribute collectively.

Wherever the discussions between Britain and the other western European countries take place and in whatever form, it is no use trying to pretend that Britain is a European country like any other, or trying to play down and dismiss as non-existent her ties with the United States and the older Commonwealth countries. (The newer Commonwealth countries are much less significant in this context.) The special relationship in the sense of some particular virtue attached to Anglo-American relations, or some particular position of privilege enjoyed by Britain at Washington, is of course a myth and sometimes a dangerous one. But the special relationship in the sense of a greater awareness in Britain of the need for America to play a permanent role in Europe and of the advantages as well as the disadvantages of close contacts with the United States is a fact, and continental statesmen are well within their rights in calling attention to it. The same is true of Britain's special relations with Canada, Australia and New Zealand which it would be folly to jettison. What Britain needs to emphasize is that these extra-European relations are a source of strength not of weakness, and that a healthy Europe, whatever degree of unity it attains, will need to find a way in which these ties can be made to work to mutual advantage.

The basic British decision of 1961 must be re-affirmed; a united Europe within the Atlantic Alliance must be the central aim of British foreign policy; what must be questioned is whether the way to get into Europe is to proclaim that we shall be ruined unless we do, and to deny that we on our side have assets both national and international which should weigh in the balance against whatever new problems our admission to a European Community would bring. One says "a European Community" advisedly. The present European Communities have come to the end of the road; there is no avoiding the direct federal solution if one is to avoid either bureaucratic stag-nation or a headlong retreat into old-style national-ism. When the federal moment comes, everything in the landscape will change. That time is not yet; but meanwhile there is quite a lot to do, both in prepar-ation for this event and for our present needs.

6

Power and Influence

THE CREATION of a European federal system has been postulated as the ultimate objective of British foreign policy. The general reaction will be that this is an extremist point of view; but this is not so. It is no more than what the leaders of all the British political parties must mean when they say that they accept the political as well as the economic objectives of the Treaty of Rome. For if a grouping of countries is to have the means of deciding in common the principal aspects of economic policy, it can only do so through political institutions in which the interests of the whole and of the units which make it up are properly represented, but in which the common interest is in the end decisive. And this is what is meant by federalism. "Supra-nationalism", which has been the preferred word, is either a mere euphemism or means of federation without democratic controls—which we have seen to be unacceptable at any rate in this country.

Europe must speak either with one voice or with many; if it is to speak with one voice (as the Common Market has done in tariff negotiations) it must be in a position to carry out policies as well as enunciate them. For this to be the case, its institutions must exercise authority and not merely influence. By saying that we accept the political implications of entry into Europe we must mean that we are prepared to see Britain eventually in the same relation to Italy as is Massachusetts to California. And when that point is reached there can be neither a British nor an Italian foreign policy any more than there can be a Massachusetts or a Californian foreign policy.

If federation be accepted as an ultimate objective it must be in the light of considerations that go beyond even the economic and technical arguments that favour a European orientation of British policy, and they must be powerful ones.

The experience of other federations will be a guide to what functions need to be allotted to the centre; though one would have to see how federations work in the contemporary world and not imagine that we could start with what the American Founding Fathers found sufficient in the eighteenth century. But history provides no guidance as to how such a federation as Europe requires can be brought about. The tactics of the existing European movement—federation by stealth or federation without tears—have been shown up by General de Gaulle and by his acolytes in other countries. And this is not surprising. No group of historic nations has ever come together voluntarily to form a federation; the cantons of Switzerland, the American colonies, the provinces of Canada, the states of Australia were never nations in the sense in which Britain, France, Germany or Italy are nations: though it is possible that Quebec may be developing into a nation within the framework of a Canadian confederation. Indeed there are more signs of centrifugal than of federating tendencies over most of the world—the linguistic struggle in Belgium is one indication—and the world scene is littered with federations that have collapsed.

Nevertheless the very existence of these tendencies towards greater local autonomy—Scottish and Welsh nationalism for instance—may be regarded as actually encouraging because they seem to show that there is no finality about the modern nation-State; the precise location of governmental powers is always an open question, and requires modification from time to time in the light of new circumstances and new demands. There may often be a case for devolution as powerful as that for the delegation of powers to a central authority; we may find before Britain enters a European federation that the appropriate units would be England, Scotland and Wales rather than Britain as such. European federation might also be the only path towards reuniting Ireland.

Centrifugal tendencies are however only one aspect of the political malaise that affects Europe and whose anti-democratic aspects are, as we have seen, a principal reason why Britain rightly fights shy of federation for the time being. We have been told that before we can come into the Common Market, we must get our house in order, by which is meant find solutions to our balance of payments problem and other apparent weaknesses in the economic structure; but political weaknesses in Britain and on the continent are no less important. The current lack of political leadership in western Europe to which de Gaulle is the only exception, suggests that our countries have not yet solved the problem of finding their new élites or of developing a new style of politics appropriate to the kind of issues that now fall to be resolved.

A circular argument confronts us here as so often in political matters. It could be claimed that Europe's problems would be less acute and dissatisfaction less rampant if we could embark upon a more rapid transformation of economic structures in the light of new technical possibilities, and that what prevents this happening is precisely the absence of a common European basis for such an enterprise. In other words,

what needs to be done to set the stage for European
union is something which only European union would
make possible. If this were true Europe, and Britain
with it, would be faced with an impasse. But it may
not be true; it may just be that there are things which
it would be easier to do if there were a central European legislature and executive but which could be
done without them. If what is needed is a European
company law to enable enterprises to ignore national
boundaries, this could be enacted by individual
countries by agreement. It might even be that with
a greater degree of managerial imagination, much
could be done—as it is already done by American-
owned enterprises—within the existing legal framework. It may even be that the unwillingness to contemplate a purely tariff arrangement between EFTA
and the Common Market because of the fear that this
would preclude Britain's eventual membership of the
latter is based upon an erroneous conception of the
likely time-scale.

Even more important may be the argument that it
is not the lagging of the growth rate of the European
economies, and its inability to be more like the United
States or to have a future in "space" that explains
Europe's present querulous state, but rather the failure
to cope more successfully with the degree of growth
that has already been achieved. There may be a fundamental maldistribution of effort, as is clearly the case
in the United States itself.

One reason for our uncertainties about these
questions is that for all the proliferation of European
institutions and organizations, public and private, the
countries of Europe still tackle their most important

problems, that is the problems with the biggest human and so political element, very much on their own, whether or not they belong to the Common Market group. Despite the lip-service paid to the European idea we still do not regard discussion of problems within a European forum as the natural course of action. Britain may be particularly blameworthy in this respect; it is not uniquely blameworthy.

Two examples may suffice. 1968 was a year of student disturbances; not only in Europe, it is true, but in Europe to an unprecedented degree. There are three elements which are common to the student problem everywhere in Europe west of the iron curtain. There has been a rate of growth of the student population which has been far too rapid by comparison with the facilities that the Universities have been able to provide. There has been a lack of policy in regard to the way in which modern Universities should hold the balance between society's need for particular skills and for the advancement of knowledge and the individual's right to personal cultural opportunity. There exists an organized international movement which for political ends of a wholly non-democratic kind has been exploiting student unrest in order to attack the foundations both of the academy and of society itself.

The last of these three is essentially a police and security problem—society cannot tolerate disruption —and it may be that the European governments are more in touch with each other and readier to learn from each other and to co-operate with each other than the ordinary citizen is in a position to know. One must hope so. But police measures, although vital, can only deal with wilful attempts at disrupting

University life. What has clearly not taken place has been any serious comparison of experience in the University field; there has been no sign of any real willingness to learn from other people's successes or failures. The governments and the University authorities in each country pursue their separate paths in isolation as though each manifestation of the problem was *sui generis*.

The other example goes still deeper. The twenty years between the two world wars were, from the social point of view, the years of mass unemployment in almost the whole of Europe outside Russia. The measures adopted by the several governments—based largely on ideas of economic autarky—made the problem worse; its psychological and political consequences are not yet exhausted. By contrast the last two decades have been years in which the expansion and redeployment of the economy of the West European countries have outrun their own supply of labour and made it necessary to recruit labour from outside. We have already noted that in Britain's case the persistence of imperial sentiment made it natural to recruit the bulk of such labour from Commonwealth countries; and have pointed to some of the difficulties to which this has given rise. But in essence—despite complicating factors of colour or religion—the basic social issues are still comparable with those of migrant labour in Europe: Italians in Switzerland, Spaniards in France; Turks and Greeks in Germany. It is true that by and large labour migration in Europe has been temporary and in Britain a prelude to settlement. But once again one is struck by the apparent failure to look at European problems as a whole. Even where there is an obvious analogy to our own version of the problem, as in the case of Holland's absorption of the Eurasian influx from Indonesia, we do not seem to have inquired whether or not the careful planning of the operation by the Dutch proved more successful than our improvisations and basically laisser-faire approach.

In the British case a natural insularity has been given greater weight by these elements in the public mind which derive ultimately from the imperial past. It comes naturally to people in Britain to feel that if there is something wrong in the world there is some kind of obligation upon Britain to put it right. Disasters, natural or man-made, evoke both greater generosity in financial response and greater willingness to offer personal services than is common in anyhow the larger European countries. "Oxfam" is a phenomenon which one could hardly imagine in any other European country—Sweden and Switzerland perhaps excepted. But such impulses are normally directed outside Europe where needs are greater and more clamant.

One should not decry the value of this phenomenon simply because it does not fit in with a European ideology. It has a double merit quite apart from the good that is actually done. It illustrates the fact that there are ways in which it is possible for a country which is no longer a great power to exercise a beneficial influence on the world, and by so doing to add to the esteem in which others hold it and to its own self-esteem, which is important. It provides a useful instead of destructive channel for the energies of sections of the population who might in earlier times have found an outlet in building or running the Empire and who find irksome the idea of settling down in early life to the humdrum world of domestic industry and commerce. Better voluntary service overseas than "demos" or drugs at home.

Nevertheless the dangers are not all imaginary. The paternalistic element in the desire to be of assistance has led to an ideology of foreign aid and to the setting up of institutions based upon this ideology, in particular the Ministry of Overseas Development. Technical co-operation between advanced and developing countries—and in more modest days we had simply a Department of Technical Co-operation—is essential to the world's economic health as it always has been, and cannot now be effective without some intergovernmental sponsorship. But to imagine that enough is known about the way societies achieve modernization and about the impact of foreign aid upon this process for a planning organization largely staffed by British academic economists to make an important contribution to it is to show a degree of confidence which it is hard to justify. Overseas aid may also be diversion of resources, physical in part but to a greater extent, intellectual, which we can doubtfully afford. The British are not unique in their activity and innocence in the aid field; but some other countries which go in for this kind of thing—notably France—do so with at least a fairly firm idea of the national interests these activities are supposed to serve. It is a sobering thought that just as financial aid to underdeveloped countries—notably in Latin America —has been less than enough to offset the effects upon them of a fall in the prices of their principal exports, so one of the main results of the technical and professional links with them has been the creaming off of part of their élite to work in the more advanced countries themselves. No-one who has seen the circumstances in which Indian doctors are supposed to work could blame them for preferring to practise in Britain; but this reverse flow of skills is hard to reconcile with any coherent strategy for dealing with the problems of the Third World.

To say these things is not being complacent or obscurantist. If there is any abidingly useful legacy of Britain's close involvement with other continents it is precisely the degree to which it is realized that the poverty and backwardness of most of the "New States" are as much a menace to world stability as the revolutionary and subversive activity which they promote, and to some extent justify. Just as the cholera epidemics of the mid-nineteenth century are held to have been the decisive factor in making the tax-paying classes ready to support measures of public sanitation —since riches gave no immunity to infection—so the wealthier parts of the world have decided they cannot ignore poverty elsewhere.

Where the analogy breaks down is that while medical science and the development of sanitary engineering pointed the correct way to dealing with the problems of urban health, no such convincing body of theory or expertise exists where mass poverty and economic stagnation are concerned. There is today much less certainty than there existed even a decade ago that we know how to go about the job, and much of the optimism that existed among professional economists has been dissipated by harsh experience. Even where aspects of the problem seem too obvious to require demonstration—the pressure of population against limited resources in food—they are sometimes dismissed as irrelevant. It is ironical indeed that the principal obstacles to encouraging on an international basis the efforts of willing governments to stem the population explosion should be the adherents of a religious body which is almost wholly dominated by the rich countries of Europe and North America.

It is therefore important that Britain and other advanced countries continue to recognize the importance of the problems of world poverty and concert together as to how the relatively limited role they can at present play in its alleviation should be performed. Where they believe solutions to these problems exist, they should not hesitate to make their views known. We are often told that it is an idle mockery to proclaim the virtues of free enterprise in countries where there exists neither capital nor an entrepreneurial class. But if we do believe that, by and large, capitalism is still the most proven instrument for the production of wealth, it is absurd to be inhibited from saying so; it might be better if more governments and ruling groups were converted to the view that if they could provide the environment in which capitalism could flourish, they would do better for their peoples than they are doing by putting their faith in a "socialism" for which they also lack the essential preconditions. The Soviet Union suffers from no such inhibitions in extolling its own preferred pattern; yet the conditions of many underdeveloped countries are almost as remote from those of Russia today or even in 1917 as from those in Western Europe or North America.

What we must avoid doing is giving aid in penny packets for projects in which we do not really believe in order to sustain governments in whose competence there can be no real trust. Present policies lead to disillusion on both sides which could lead to an unnecessary bitterness.

It is hardly necessary to add that an even greater rigour should be applied to controlling arms deliveries, whether on terms that make them a form of aid or in respect of commercial transactions. Arms supplies from Britain to various Middle Eastern potentates have not produced the promised dividends in political stability, and the same miscalculations as to how arms would be used and what is meant by "defence" are perhaps being made in respect of new States in Africa. One need not share the left-wing mythology about wicked arms manufacturers to hold the view that in a world where so many governments profess violence or at least condone it as a means to political objectives, advanced countries must consider the politics of the arms trade as something germane to their central preoccupation with stability. Here there is yet another realm of policy in which there seems to have been no real effort to arrive at a European consensus.

Some people might wish where Africa is concerned to go further still. There is mounting evidence of the inability of either anglophone or francophone Africa to develop political stability sufficient for programmes of development to make the headway they need in order to minimize the opportunities for trouble-making by Soviet or Chinese trained communists. It is dangerous therefore that there should enter into the picture any continuation of the rivalries between the ex-colonial powers, whether motivated by political or commercial considerations. In their relations with the Common Market some Commonwealth African countries have shown that they will follow the path that seems dictated to them by their own economic interests, and the same is obviously true of their politics. It would therefore be absurd to say that the old line between the colonial empires should be regarded as sacrosanct under the new conditions. The important thing—since the enthusiasm of the United States for involvement in African affairs is waning—is that there should be agreement among the European nations as to what if any their actions should be, when faced by the African countries and their feuds, external and internal. As in so many other aspects of Britain's relations with Europe, this means first and foremost a meeting of minds between Britain and France. It is another example of the hollowness of the notion that French policy can be ignored or circumvented by arrangements with the "other five".

It is not only in respect of such external issues that one must regret that the pursuit of an undefined post-imperial role has led Britain to neglect the possibilities open to her as part of Europe. There is also the consequent failure to perceive the extent to which Europe itself presents challenges both to the gifted and enterprising, and to those with an alert social conscience. The frontiers of Europe are sometimes still in Europe; some of them are in the British Isles. One is familiar with the argument that the difficulties which the United States faces are due to its having over-extended itself in the degree of its commitment to the universal containment of Communism. Those in

America who preach what is sometimes called neo-isolationism do so partly because they fear that the result of failure overseas—for example in Viet Nam —may lead the pendulum to swing too far in the other direction, and to the neglect of areas where the American presence is essential—Europe, for instance. The same may be said of a plea for some degree of British neo-isolationism as a prelude to a final coming to terms with the movement for a United Europe.

A main source of a country's strength today—if it is out of the great power league—lies in it being able to demonstrate that nothing it undertakes is beyond its capacity. Britain by contrast has clearly attempted far too much, has suffered far too many set-backs, and now gives an image of impotent fussiness instead of calm assurance. Not only foreign secretaries may lack dignity to the country's detriment; foreign policies can lack dignity also.

Dignity should not be confused with complacency. Complacency is indeed Britain's besetting vice; and the complacency of the Left over the retreat from Empire is far greater than the complacency of the Right over the methods by which it was created. Britain has not, it is true, fought two fatal rearguard actions as did France in Indo-China and Algeria. Aden is pretty small beer by comparison. But there have been three bloody and so far unfinished wars in the wake of Britain's withdrawal; Indians and Pakistanis, Jews and Arabs, Nigerians and Biafrans. We are openly threatened with another along the line of the Zambesi, and we cannot yet be confident of the future of Malaysia and Singapore. More lives—though not British lives —will have been lost in winding up the Empire than were lost in the fighting which accompanied its growth.

So let us not pretend that the record of withdrawal is a glorious one or that it commands from others the respect it gets at home. It should rather serve as a warning against being over-stretched either materially or intellectually. It is of course the case that the ragged edges of British foreign policy today are the consequence of events for which the present generation of policy-makers are not responsible. Britain is landed with the debris of an Empire and a consequent dispersal of effort. There are populations in territories coveted by others which we cannot in decency surrender; the Falkland Islands because we do not wish to surrender a wholly British population to a country as poorly governed and as intolerant and xenophobic as Argentina; Gibraltar because of the nature of the Spanish regime that claims it. Yet in every other respect good relations with both Argentina and Spain —whatever their regimes—are dictated by all material considerations of self-interest. British Honduras and even Guyana, despite its status as an independent member of the Commonwealth—present analogous situations; though perhaps the goodwill of Guatemala might be regarded as something with which one could dispense, were it not for the lurking shadow of that fantastic relic of the early nineteenth century—the Monroe doctrine.

It is of course difficult in such situations to make plain the reasons for the policy that Britain tries to follow: fidelity to the principle of self-determination combined with an unwillingness to enlarge the area of conflict with the other countries involved. As we have seen, the atmosphere of the United Nations is not conducive to impartiality in any dispute in which Britain is involved. As a result one gets an impression of irresolution and of playing things down which does the country no good. Similar pussy-footing has marked some of Britain's handling of cases of injustice to British citizens abroad. The long detention of the British pilots in whose plane the Congolese leader Tshombe was kidnapped is a case in point. But this does not only apply to semi-barbarous regimes like that of Algeria which seems since independence to have taken up its old role as the headquarters of the barbary corsairs against whom the fledgling American navy did much sterling work in Thomas Jefferson's day. There have also been incidents involving more considerable countries, notably the Soviet Union. The trouble here may not be simple disregard for the ordinary principles of law, but a code of laws different from those which prevail in other western countries, and differences of legal procedure which may bear harshly on the foreigner. British people, prepared to travel anywhere and do anything, may be particularly liable to create difficulties for their own government.

The dilemma is obvious once more. The age of gunboat diplomacy being past does one swallow one's pride and accept the maltreatment of British citizens, or does one elevate such incidents into a diplomatic dispute with the country concerned?

One must distinguish between different kinds of cases. Where there are allegations of espionage or subversion behind the iron curtain, it is necessary to trust the Government to do what it can, since it alone knows the facts. In other cases public clamour may be easier to justify. The difficulty is in part that we have to deal with regimes for whom some individual rights that we cherish are meaningless. For instance there have for a long time been cases in which the Russians have refused to allow Russian women to marry British subjects who have met them while residing in Russia. This is because the Soviet regime specifically denies any right of expatriation to its citizens. And the same is true of other Communist countries.

These problems merge into the wider one of the degree to which there should be official expressions of opinion, or even unofficial expressions of opinion which some foreign governments are likely to regard as officially sponsored, concerning the internal regimes of foreign countries or their maltreatment of their own citizens. Such issues arise at both ends of the political spectrum—in respect of the Soviet Union and the countries which it dominates and in respect of allied Governments such as the "Colonels' regime" in Greece. There is no easy answer. It is wrong that Britain by silence should appear to condone tyranny; it is idle to talk, if talk is all.

One must take into account the fact that what remains of British prestige abroad, particularly perhaps behind the iron curtain, largely depends upon the belief that her own citizens enjoy an unusual measure of personal freedom. It is important that this reputation should remain intact, and that it should be expounded as being based upon principles universally applicable. To a limited extent international action is possible, but again primarily on a European basis. The legal machinery for dealing with human rights within the framework of the Council of Europe is important both for its own sake and as an example of what could be done on a wider scale as between civilized governments. It stands in conspicuous contrast to the failure of the United Nations to make anything of "human rights" as a subject for action.

Most depends however upon what happens in Britain—both in respect of the treatment which aliens receive and in respect of the legal safeguards for the rights of British citizens themselves. In this respect the Home Office is no less involved in foreign policy than the Foreign Office. For there exists in Britain, despite the very real traditional legal safeguards such as *habeas corpus*, a degree of arbitrariness on some matters which have historically been considered essentially executive—all, for instance, that relates to passports and to entry into the country. This is one of the areas into which the *Ombudsman*—the Parliamentary Commissioner—is precluded from entering. It looks as though one could add to the usual argument for improving the citizen's prospect of getting justice from the State something relating to the repercussions of this arbitrariness upon foreign and Commonwealth relations.

The presence of a domestic frontier which needs bringing within the scope of fully civilized existence applies with even greater force to the problems of the coloured immigrant community and their British-born offspring. It is no good going over the circumstances in which the problem was allowed to grow up or the excuses, harder to find, for the delay in looking at its implications, and in framing appropriate policies. Whatever may be true of the past, the existence of palpable disadvantages of a material kind in one section of a country's population when that country enjoys the affluence of contemporary Britain is unnecessary and intolerable. The prejudices and resentments to which it gives rise and which are often magnified in the telling are a blot upon Britain's reputation and so a handicap upon her foreign policy. Legislation may do something towards remedying some grievances; others will hardly respond to legislation particularly in a country where individual rights have been prescriptive rather than the fruits of positive enactment. Nor can prejudice be removed by legislation; though legislative norms may help as the history of the removal of religious disabilities surely illustrates. So long as there is acute competition for scarce resources in the housing and educational fields, trouble is inevitable. Only positive and deliberately discriminatory expenditure, and effort on a scale hitherto not envisaged, can make a real impact upon the situation; and the same is true of other sections of the population who have not shared in the general rise in prosperity.

All this is very far from the traditional concerns of the makers of foreign policy, and it would be wrong to particularize in greater detail the nature of the reforms in the running of Britain's internal affairs which require to be made before the country recovers a sense of community in which all can share. Neo-isolationism should not be confused with a parochial Little Englandism which would limit the rights and benefits of the constitution to the true-born Englishman—an individual upon the idea of whose existence, Daniel Defoe cast mocking doubt more than two and half centuries ago. We now have to include Indians,

Pakistanis and West Indians alongside the descendants of earlier migrations, from those of the Anglo-Saxons on. British pride in the post-imperial era cannot be a pride of race and must therefore be a pride in the ideas and institutions which together make up the notion we have of Britain and its meaning to the world. And one uses the word pride advisedly, since it is the lack of pride in Britain's achievements and potential—the consequence in part of errors in the past and in part of an anti-national current of thought among an influential part of the intelligentsia—that is a large part of our difficulties.

It must not be thought that we are falling back into the trap of neglecting the role of power—even of military power—in relations between states, and saying that influence is enough. What one is saying is that the ability to use to best advantage the relatively restricted power which Britain now has at its disposal will depend to a very great extent upon ability to use her influence within the complicated structure of alliances and other institutional ties which are now the condition of prosperity and security in the wider world arena. And this in turn depends upon it being seen that the objectives that British policy seeks are well within her reach and that the government that pursues them can rely upon the support of a united national community.

It may seem that this conclusion enshrines a paradox, as it suggests that the way to proceed to a non-national solution of Britain's problems is through the pursuit of self-regarding national goals. But such a view would be mistaken for two reasons. It assumes that the federal or European solution is near at hand, whereas a more realistic survey of the scene would suggest that it is very far off; and it is imperative to do what can be done now. It also assumes that a satisfactory basis for union can be found in countries that are themselves weak and a prey to self-doubt. It would appear more likely that the contrary is the case. If Britain is divided between the energetic and enterprising who feel so hemmed in that they seek or are tempted to seek the path of emigration as the way to self-fulfilment, and the majority who remain behind in a mood of surly scepticism—or, where the young are concerned, of wild, irrational and dangerously hate-filled utopianism—then it cannot take the lead in bringing about those institutional innovations that are essential if the European bark is to be rescued from its present becalmed state. There need be no contradiction—General de Gaulle's dissent notwithstanding—between a healthy Europeanism and a healthy nationalism.

It remains to be seen whether the framework of British institutions and the current disposition of political forces in Britain permit one to hope that the desirable is also the possible.

7

The Making of
British Foreign Policy

THE APPROPRIATE foreign policy for Britain must
be one which is based upon a measure of agreement
transcending the existing political parties, as it
demands a degree of continuity in approach and effort
which could not be restricted to the lifetime of an
administration or a parliament. It is also, as we have
seen, very closely related to domestic policies which
themselves are of a long-range kind. Despite the fact
that fairly tight limits are set by the external environment, especially the economic environment, to what
a British government can do, so that any incoming
government, (however fresh its standpoint) is likely to
end up with the same restricted number of choices as
its predecessor, there is a difference between a positive
reaction to the challenge of circumstance and a mere
carrying on with current business.

In the distant past, the continuity of foreign policy
was largely a result of the narrowness of the circle
within which foreign policy was formulated, and of
the general assumption that it was essentially an executive matter not normally suited to parliamentary
or public debate. With the nineteenth-century widen-
ing of the franchise and the growth of an educated
public outside the narrowly political arena interested
in foreign affairs for commercial or idealistic reasons,
the need to take it into the confidence of rulers was
more generally recognized; and, even more important,
those who dissented from a given line of policy
(whether over the American civil war in the 1860s
or the Balkans in the 1870s) felt no compunction
about taking their case to the public.

But the kind of issues that lent themselves to public

debate were generally those which had a high quota of moral content and were not necessarily central to the country's fortunes. The great transformation at the turn of this century was carried through largely in private by governments of different political complexions with little consultation with Parliament, and relatively little general discussion.

One of the reasons for the popularity of the League of Nations idea in Britain was that it would enable foreign policy to be conducted in the open, and thus more in accordance with current democratic assumptions. And although the League disappointed its supporters in many respects, it remained true that after 1919, foreign policy did figure to a larger extent than previously in the ordinary discussions about British politics. It had ceased to be the preserve of a narrow political élite. On the other hand there remained a considerable degree of continuity between governments. Continuity was not complete. The Lloyd George coalition fell directly, and the first MacDonald government indirectly, over issues of foreign policy, but since no government other than a Conservative government enjoyed a clear majority in the inter-war period, it is perhaps not surprising that the differences were those of emphasis rather than of substance.

An additional factor making for continuity had entered into the picture by this time, namely the Foreign Office and its professional staff. Until the beginning of the twentieth century foreign policy was made by ministers and notably by the Foreign Secretary himself, subject to the overriding influence of the Prime Minister on such topics as he chose for his intervention. The Foreign Secretary's advisers were often the ambassadors in the field who themselves were often *grands seigneurs* (at the major posts) with social and hence political influence at home.

During the foreign secretaryship of Edward Grey in the years immediately preceding the First World War, the foreign office developed its modern organiz- ation no longer as a mere instrument of the Foreign Secretary occupied in the copying and filing of dis- patches but as a source of expert advice, funnelled through the Permanent Under-Secretary. The Foreign Service too became increasingly a professional career service, though only gradually shedding its previously aristocratic connotations. While uniformity of view was not to be expected, an "office view" did tend to grow up, and was bound to be particularly influential in any area towards which an incumbent Foreign Secretary could not find time to turn his attention. The amalgamation of the Foreign Office staff and the Diplomatic Service after 1919 further increased the cohesiveness and consequently the influence of the official world.

After the Second World War it was again expected that some radical innovation in the handling of inter- national relations would come about, and in some quarters it was assumed that the new Labour govern- ment, the first such government to have a parliamen- tary majority, would be able to set Britain on a new course. It was hoped in such quarters that socialism would be a binding element and that "Left would speak to Left". The reasons for the frustration of these hopes are too familiar to bear repetition. The wartime alliance for mutual convenience between the West and the Soviet Union was shown to have no ideological basis and did nothing to heal the breach between the Second International and the formally defunct Third International and its far from defunct constituent parties. The Soviet definition of a socialist partner was one which would give at all times un-questioned adherence to the Soviet viewpoint; no elected British government—Labour or not—was likely to be that docile.

Ernest Bevin thus followed a foreign policy which, given the circumstances, could only be described as highly traditionalist and wholly in accord with the views of the "office", among whose personnel he achieved a reputation all the greater because of the misgivings which had been felt about his advent beforehand. Unfortunately this meeting of minds ex-tended not only to Bevin's undoubtedly correct Atlantic policy but also to his much more questionable suspicion of the movement for European unity, and his very dubious and highly partisan policy in the Middle East where the established pro-Arab and anti-Zionist prejudices of much of British officialdom were given free rein.

Although there was dissent from Bevin's policy in all three areas, both in the Labour Party and among the Opposition, its disparate elements with their differ-ent motivations never fused. And the same thing has remained true of foreign policy in the twenty years since Bevin left the Foreign Office. There has been a mainstream irrespective of party, together with vary-ing counter-currents.

The inability of dissent over foreign policy to be more effective springs from causes at once political and institutional. Let us take the political ones first.

The factions that have been in opposition—excluding only the period during which the Labour Party under Gaitskell's leadership was in its majority opposed to entry to the Common Market—have on the whole been weakened by their utopianism: the lack of any sufficiently coherent and realistic view of the world into which the policies they advocated could be fitted.

Such utopianism has been as true of the Right as of the Left. The surviving advocates of a specifically imperialist approach to British policy—the Suez group as they became for a time after 1954—were hampered not only by the lack of any broad public response to the idea of clinging onto Empire, but also by their opposition to close ties with the United States and their inability to accept American opposition to trade discrimination and consequently to Commonwealth preferences. The alternative they would have preferred —closer economic ties with the Commonwealth based upon preferential trade arrangements—was no longer possible, if it ever had been, given as we have seen the changing trade patterns and interests of the Common-wealth countries themselves.

On the Left, the nuclear disarmers, the opponents of NATO and those who wanted a neutralist Britain were postulating a world which did not exist, as they assumed that the "Cold War" was a something which had been deliberately initiated by the West, and could be called off by the West at will, instead of being the inevitable result of the policies pursued by the Soviet Union. Nevertheless the appeal of such a rejection of power politics remained considerable, and was enhanced by the horrors of the Viet Nam war. The

"New Left" of the last few years has thus had an outlook on foreign policy which, without offering a constructive ideal except in so far as revolutionary mysticism centred round a China or a Cuba—both equally unknown in their concrete manifestations—can be said to provide one, has one basic negative foundation—namely a total repudiation of and hatred for the United States.

Most of the "New Left" would deny that they are pro-Soviet simply because they are anti-American; but it cannot be denied that since there is no choice for Britain except that between an alignment with the United States and a subservience to the Soviet Union, the objective result of destroying public confidence in the United States is to improve the chances of the Soviet Union attaining its foreign policy aims. Indeed, many of the attitudes and slogans of the New Left are parallel to those of the Soviet Union—such as its intense hostility, for instance, to the German Federal Republic and to Israel. Only the Soviet Union's own wooden fears of any revolutionary movement over which it cannot itself exercise total control can explain its hostility to this phenomenon.

The element in British opinion—inside and outside the Labour Party—which is committed to a pro-Soviet orientation has remained small, but is not for that reason to be dismissed as negligible and is certainly not to be equated with the tiny percentage of the electorate that votes Communist. This element is not of course open to the charge of utopianism, since subservience to the Soviet Union is a possible fate for Britain as indeed for any country from which, for one reason or another, the United States is prepared to withdraw its overt or implicit guarantee of independence.

In between the extremes of dissent there has been a central body of opinion which has followed with very little trouble in the wake of the political leadership of the principal political parties. There has been, as we have noted, only one issue on which there has been a serious measure of disagreement in the country; and that has been on whether to seek entry into the Common Market. The handling of this question illustrates the difficulty of trying to occupy a half-way house between an élitist and a democratic control of foreign policy.

Despite the fact that there was a European movement in existence with considerable following and a fairly well-defined ideology, the moves by which the institutions of the Six were initiated on the continent were largely left to a small political and bureaucratic group in the countries concerned; and no effort was made to consult popular wishes or to give Parliaments more than a ratifying role. The bureaucratic character of the Brussels machinery was thus implicit in its creation. The first British attempt at entry was due to the conversion of important figures in Whitehall and of some Conservative politicians to the view that British economic interests were more likely to benefit by admission than by exclusion. They also attempted to treat the matter as a largely technical one and to avoid anything in the nature of a large-scale public debate, but the attempt failed as the parties were not prepared to accept the policy on trust. An important minority in the Conservative party and an actual majority in the Labour Opposition of the time made their hostility plain. As a result the continental advocates of Britain's membership had their hands weakened by the evidence given by Britain's negotiating team of their need, all the time, to find ways of conciliating hostile or sceptical opinion at home. Given the apparent state of British opinion as a whole, the first de Gaulle veto was not so unreasonable.

The Labour Party, in office and with Gaitskell dead, then accepted the policy it had previously opposed—since the Gaitskellite conditions amounted to rejection—and made the second attempt at entry. Although there had by now been more debate so that the issues —at least the economic issues—were better understood, it was still far from clear that there was a consensus, even though the Government were in a better position than the Macmillan government had been in, as the Conservative opposition was on the whole favourable to the enterprise. Dissent still existed and the lobby in favour of NAFTA that sprang up after the second de Gaulle veto was largely identical—in both its Labour and Conservative wings—with the previous anti-Common Market grouping.

Not only is it improper in a country which professes to be a democracy that a major and probably irrevocable decision should be reached without full public debate, but it is inefficient that things should be done in this way. It stores up trouble for the future. Nor is this the only instance that could be given of a seeming unwillingness to take the public into the confidence of the Government where important issues of foreign policy are concerned. Sometimes a Government will appear to act in a way which sharply contradicts the apparent trend of public opinion. For instance

the strongly pro-Israeli feeling in the country at the
time of the Six Day War in 1967—to which the
opinion polls gave ample testimony—was not reflected
in British diplomacy which continued along its traditional pro-Arab lines, fortified no doubt by the
personal preferences of Britain's representative at the
United Nations, Lord Caradon. Sometimes, as over
Viet Nam, the Government may take unpopular posi-
tions for reasons which are perfectly valid perhaps
but which it is unwilling to disclose or discuss.

A principal reason for such discrepancies and
silences is the institutional one. The basic mechanism
of the modern British constitution—responsible party
government—was well into its stride before foreign
policy was admitted to be subject to the same rules as
domestic matters. But although it was inevitable that
it should be so admitted there were disadvantages
which have not yet been overcome.

The British system rests upon a battle between
"ins" and "outs" with the "outs" using the opportunities afforded by Parliamentary debate to discredit
the "ins" and so to prepare the way to replacing them.
The result is that issues are chosen for debate—and
in this, Parliament gives a lead to the press and the
country—not so much because of their intrinsic importance as according to whether or not their ventil-
ation serves a party purpose. The existence of rival
parties tends to make matters which should be neutral
in themselves a subject of controversy and to force
people to take sides not according to the merits of the
particular issue but according to their allegiance
to government or opposition respectively. Furthermore
opposition can always be dismissed as irresponsible or

ill-informed because of the monopoly which the Government exercises over the principal sources of information which are those at the disposal of officialdom.

It can be asked whether this matters very much. Since policy has in the end to be executed by those who make it, can one do more than give the government of the day the benefit of the doubt? Is it not likely that an Opposition taking office will discover that it is subject to the same compulsions as its predecessor, and come round to their views on most important matters? The acceptance by the Labour leadership of the desirability of entering the Common Market will be adduced as a good recent example. Against this must be set the fact that if an Opposition carries its campaign to the extent of pledging itself to a reversal of policy on any important external issue, it will not only create confusion in the public mind at home but also raise hopes abroad that it may not be able to fulfil. A case in point would be the current statements by Conservative leaders that they intend to reverse the present Government's policy of withdrawal from East of Suez. While one may sympathize with their feelings about the decision and still more about the reasons for it, there are obvious dangers in persuading the Commonwealth governments in the area that they can afford in framing their own policies, to ignore the British decision because it is not going to be implemented. And how can they be certain that the Conservatives will be returned to power in time?

The perception of this weakness has led to a now familiar debate about the desirability of some kind of external affairs committee in Parliament on the lines of what exists in most important foreign legislatures. It is held that this would create within Parliament a body of informed opinion which in turn would improve the standard of parliamentary debate and so of the public discussion of questions of foreign policy. In support of this view it is truthfully claimed that the operations of the relevant committees of the American Congress do promote a much more genuine and far-ranging debate when American policy is undergoing one of its major crises than we ever get in this country. Against this it is fair to add that in foreign policy, as in other fields, the greater power that Congress exercises (as compared with a British-type parliament) provides a bigger handle for domestic pressure groups, by which either to obstruct a particular policy or to secure some narrow objective of their own at the price of that policy's general coherence.

The real objections in Britain to this idea do not however spring from fears that this danger would be repeated; British pressure groups are less well-entrenched—some American ones scarcely have a British parallel—and there are ways of limiting what they can do. The main obstacle comes from the realization of the fact that there would be no purpose in having such a committee unless it were empowered to hear testimony from officials as well as ministers. This would modify the conventional relationship between minister and civil servant to a greater extent than most people in Whitehall would desire; it would also involve making available to ordinary members of Parliament information which officials would find it more comfortable—and Ministers also—to keep to themselves. The opposition put up by the Foreign Office to the quite reasonable suggestion that the existing select committee on agriculture should visit Brussels and find out for itself what entry into the Common Market would in fact involve for British farming, is evidence enough of how deep these fears can go.

The other principal objection is the simple one that Ministers do not see what they have to gain from such a committee compared with the possible limitations upon their freedom of action which its existence and the publicity of the arguments to which its work might give rise would inevitably entail. Ministers are dedicated to the view that foreign policy is better carried on as privately as possible, and that the less they offer which the Opposition can attack the better placed they will be. Why add to their already considerable burdens that of discussing their policies with a committee which would be largely composed of their political opponents? It is, in other words, the difference in the constitutional setting between Britain and the United States that makes the idea of a foreign affairs committee so unlikely to be accepted. If one has, as in the United States, a separation of powers with a legislature that cannot be controlled through party discipline but which has to be carried along largely by the exercise of persuasion, the Executive branch has no option but to make what efforts are needed. In Britain, with its normally assured governmental majority, Ministers have not felt the urge to secure support in this painful and time-consuming fashion.

It is sometimes thought that some disadvantages

could be avoided if the Committee's proceedings were private; but this would not suit the Opposition spokesmen who would not wish to be precluded from criticizing the Government through their having information not available to the rank and file of their own party. Opposition leaders have always been chary, for this reason, of confidential discussion with Ministers except at times of grave national emergency. And they are also of course unwilling to do anything to weaken themselves once they are in power. It is thus difficult to see anything likely to be done by Government— and Parliament can only change its procedures at the Government's bidding—to alter the present handling of foreign affairs.

It is true that the performance of Parliament as a guide to the national debate about foreign policy could be improved without the introduction of specialist committees. It is not necessary that such time as is devoted to the subject should be so largely given over to peripheral issues, and it may simply be that Parliament only reflects the inability of most recent Foreign Secretaries to explain their purposes in terms of some general conception of Britain's place in the world. For the ability of members of parliament to inform themselves on the substance of most issues does not depend upon their having information from official sources, either through a committee or obtained in some other way. The political parties, themselves, the press and various specialized bodies—whether partisan or not—can all help. And what is true of the MP, is also true of the citizen.

Compared with any past period the opportunities for the British citizen of getting to know something of the background of foreign policy are very plentiful. The danger is that the information may be misleadingly accessible, and this is particularly the case with television which is by far the commonest way in which the external world is now mediated. Television now brings instant history into the living room, particularly in its more dramatic aspects. But the effect of this exposure in terms of understanding policy does not depend solely on the skill or courage of the cameraman. The implications of events have to be discussed and explored and for this television rarely provides the time. As a result, important questions are treated with such brevity as to leave the viewer with the impression that things are much simpler than is in fact the case. The hyper-sensitivity of political parties to policy discussions not under their own auspices means that most television and radio discussion concentrates on the interpretation of events abroad rather than on the question of what British policy should be, thus fortifying the tendency, recently noted by a foreign student of Britain's foreign policy, to think of it as a series of responses to particular questions rather than as something coherent to be defined by its own goals.

It is also hard in a major institution like the BBC to get away from the current orthodoxies of the intelligentsia which may be as constraining as those of the "Establishment" itself. It is easy to wax indignant about government monopoly of the mass-media in totalitarian countries and of radio and television even in Gaullist France. But there can also be distortion when you have on the one hand a tacit conspiracy between the main political parties, and on the other hand the innate conformism of an intelligentsia.

The role of the press in creating public opinion on foreign affairs again depends as much on its treatment of news as on the expression of opinions; though the opinions of some journals do weigh with policy-makers. It seems generally agreed that Britain has no single newspaper with as good a serious coverage of foreign affairs as *Le Monde,* or a magazine as capable of launching a debate on basic issues as influential as the American *Foreign Affairs.* But given the range of newspapers and other publications available to the British citizen, he is probably better off in respect of information on foreign policy questions than most other people. He would be better off still, if many newspapers did not follow the bad example of the foreign service itself, in rotating their correspondents too frequently for them to acquire the deep and personalized knowledge of a foreign country, its language and culture which can alone give depth to any interpretation of its policies.

But all this is in the end only the raw material for political leadership to mould. Foreign policy cannot emanate from the electorate. In this field more than in any other the citizen is in the last resort dependent upon Government; if it blunders either in the selection of goals or in their execution, there is little he can do to put things right—even if he has to pay with his life for their blunders.

The organization of the British government for the purposes of foreign affairs is thus a subject of direct consequence for policy and not just a matter for the technicians of public administration. We may briefly recall the trends of development in recent decades. The most important of these have been concerned with inducing a sense of cohesion between all the departments and individuals involved in foreign policy in the broadest sense, whether their approach is the economic, the political or the military. Both the relations between departments and individual careers have been involved in this process. On the departmental side, there has been the elaboration of the system of inter-departmental committees at various levels crowned by a Cabinet committee—now the Defence and Overseas Policy Committee—in which for practical purposes the ultimate authority rests. On the personnel side there has been an effort to see that those who are likely to reach the higher posts in either the civil or the military hierarchies are adequately conversant with each other's problems and modes of thought. The work of the Imperial Defence College is the most obvious example in this field.

It is by no means self-evident that this process has been carried far enough. While the roles of the military and the civilian can never be identical, the separation between the diplomatic service and the home civil service becomes increasingly hard to justify when one realizes how many departments are constantly being affected in their own work by considerations arising out of relations with foreign countries. And if the argument that Britain's destiny is a European one be accepted, the border line between domestic and foreign affairs will be blurred still further. It would clearly be impossible to say that all servants of the State must be prepared to serve overseas, and there are specific functions of a diplomatic kind for which the expertise required is not the same as that for most civil servants. But it is equally true that within the diplomatic service the needs of specialization are beginning to be given greater recognition again. What one envisages is a uniformly recruited and administered government service within which individuals would opt for a greater or lesser degree of availability for service abroad. It may well be that the Fulton and Duncan Committees will be the last which will be asked to look at the two aspects of government service separately. The division is one which reflects the past rather than the future.

The other principal trend now reaching its culmination has been that looking to the elimination of the distinction from the administrative point of view between Commonwealth countries and the rest of the world, so that external relations come to be handled by a single department, as in other Commonwealth countries. Although this is to some extent a matter of form the reorganization will have the practical consequence of making it easier for foreign policy to be looked at regionally than it has been in the past; anglophone with francophone Africa; Malaya with Burma and Thailand and so forth.

But administration, however efficiently organized, remains the servant of policy. Officials can suggest and criticize; it is for ministers to decide. The lack of clarity in British foreign policy reflects the weaknesses of a party system which no longer corresponds to real divisions in the country and which consequently fails to present the country with the choices that it has to make. The task before Britain, if the analysis of these pages is acceptable, is so far-reaching in its implications for every aspect of British government and British life that it is doubtful if it can be carried through by either of the present competitors for power in the British political arena, or indeed under any circumstances in which the national interest is subordinated to the gaining or retention of power within the present party framework.

But that should not preclude attempts to understand the nature of the task. We have seen that the successive attempts to marry the political with the economic imperatives of British policy have come to grief, and there is no prospect that they will suddenly come together. From the political point of view the essential requirement is the maintenance in some form of the Atlantic Alliance without which the necessary degree of stability in Europe cannot be preserved. Within the Alliance however one would hope that developments in Eastern Europe and inside the Soviet Union would ultimately permit a search for new arrangements that would lower the degree of tension between East and West and permit a scaling down by mutual agreement of the burden of armaments. Within this framework the economic and technical advantages of increasing contact between the two halves of divided Europe could make themselves felt.

As we have seen, Britain can here only fulfil a modest role, and the role should be largely a matter of diplomacy within the Alliance rather than one of seeking to act independently outside it. It means particular attention to three countries; the United States, first and foremost, because only in so far as the United States and the Soviet Union can reach agreement is major progress possible; West Germany because it is the problem of divided Germany that has produced different perspectives on the part of the

German government, and still more in German public opinion, from those of the rest of the Alliance; and it is necessary to reach a greater degree of understanding before further steps can be taken; and finally, France. Without France, the Atlantic Alliance is largely void of meaning as a political instrument in addition to the handicap that France's abstention imposes upon its integrated military organization. But the importance of France to Britain is not confined to the Alliance or to Europe. An understanding with France of as complete a kind as possible should be the most immediate objective of any British government.

On the economic side, we have seen that despite the unprecedented activity of governments in encouraging and channelling trade the decisive factors have remained the economic ones themselves. Changing technologies, and differential advantages in quality and price, have continued to make themselves felt despite all distortions. The result has been, as has been shown, an almost unbroken increase in the importance of Britain's trade with Western Europe in respect both of the Common Market, and of the EFTA countries. Given the likelihood and the desirability from the general point of view of the more advanced countries specializing in the products of advanced technology, this tendency to trade with a neighbouring group of advanced industrial economies is both inevitable and desirable.

It is therefore a vital task of British diplomacy to see that whatever special arrangements exists between groups of countries of this kind should not be to the detriment of Britain's competitive position. If this means accepting association between the Common Market and EFTA (which was after all, Britain's first choice a decade ago) there should be no objection in principle.

On the other hand, Britain cannot afford to ignore the possibilities of other markets which offer a potential for growth, whether we think of the current surge in demand in Australia, or of opportunities that may eventually open up in the Soviet Union or elsewhere in Eastern Europe. We require an economic diplomacy geared to second the efforts of British industrialists and traders themselves of a no less intensive kind than that of our competitors.

It would nevertheless be wrong to imagine that the entire advanced world (capitalist and communist) can afford simply to develop its own internal economic arrangements, with no attention to their repercussions upon the poorer and more populous parts of the globe. But this again is a field where action by Britain alone can do little, except in this case provide markets for a few small dependencies—Hong Kong for instance —and where real remedial action can only be the product of co-operation as a minimum between the members of OECD.

But these are all questions of the immediate future. In the long term, the logic of the argument that the European nation state is for many purposes obsolescent is unanswerable. In the long run, therefore, Britain's aim must be to assume the position of leadership in Europe which she rejected almost a quarter-century ago, and to come out as an advocate of a European federal system as the ultimate objective of policy. But it must be clear that this is a long-term objective only.

Its economic, social, political and psychological foundations do not exist, either in Britain or on the continent. The Common Market itself is not an approach to this objective but rather a detour on the road. In all that we do, we must keep the European idea in mind but at the moment since neither the potential membership nor the appropriate institutions can be clearly seen, it would be folly to try to take short cuts.

It cannot then be said that the task is not a demanding one. Such confidence as one has must derive from the fact that England's relations to the world are no more doubtful and precarious under Elizabeth II than they were under Elizabeth I; and yet the country came through.

Index

71
72
74
75
76
77
79

83

85

88